Shatteri

A Lawyer Explains the Abortio
Abortion's So

For Laymen, Lawyer:

ISBN 9781091380844

Table of Contents:

Dedication

Cover Designer Biography and Author Biography

Works Cited

Dedication

To all the Christian warriors. To those who fight. "...[H]e that hath no sword, let him sell his garment, and buy one." – Jesus Christ, Luke 22:38

To my wife.

To my mom.

And to my wife's mom and dad. No less my family than hers.

Author Biography: Matthew S. Thomas, Esquire

Matthew Thomas is a successful attorney and political scientist. He humbly begs that neither of these be held against him.

When not reading or writing a book, Matthew practices law and helps to elect conservative candidates to public office. He is also fluent in Spanish.

Matthew's hobbies include Olympic and Viking-style fencing (sword fighting), American History, and spending time with his wife and family in beautiful Erie, PA.

If you wish to read regular political commentary from the author, please follow The Upbeat Conservative on Facebook and Twitter at https://www.facebook.com/The-Upbeat-Conservative-122526687933491 and https://twitter.com/upbeatconserv. If you want to financially support our mission to continue publishing conservative content, you can do so by going to https://www.patreon.com/UConservative and making a donation.

Cover Design by Whitney Leckenby

Whitney Leckenby is a brilliant young graphic designer from Lacey, Washington. A devoted Catholic (and devoted owner of pomeranian pooches) Whitney enjoys spending time with her many brothers, sisters, cousins, and friends.

Whitney also suffers from a rare connective tissue disease known as Fibrodysplasia ossificans progressiva, or FOP. This disease causes muscle and other soft tissue in the body to turn to bone, especially when injured (or when surgery is attempted to remove the excess bone). Recent developments in FOP research and in clinical drug tests on human patients have led to significant progress in slowing unwanted bone-growth, and it is hoped that the Food and Drug Administration will soon give full approval for these new treatments. However, a cure for the disease is still badly needed. To learn more, or to donate to FOP research efforts, visit www.ifopa.org.

FOP research involves a rather tight-knit community and group of professionals, and the reader can have confidence that their money will be put to good use.

1.

Conclusion – Yes, I'm Putting it at the Beginning

I'm putting the conclusion at the beginning of the book because, if you don't read it now, you might hate me before the end (I'm putting it at the end too – it's a great way to get away with writing less!). Of course, what do I care if you don't like me? You already bought the book.

What? You're reading Amazon's free sample, or reading this in a bookstore? Shame on you. In my religion, stealing is a sin. I'll let it slide, though. You need the information contained in these pages if you're going to be a pro-life advocate (or if you're not yet convinced). I've made sure to get most of that information from *liberal* media outlets and studies, so that it cannot be questioned based on any alleged conservative bias.

But on to the conclusion.

I know it seems like I've been hard on liberals and Democrats in this book. I have. The reason is because I want them to repent of the evil that they've been doing or supporting (and yes, because occasionally we should have a good laugh over the absurdity of their ideas – if you don't learn to laugh, you'll only ever cry, especially over a topic like this one).

The truth is that the Gospel of Jesus Christ – in which I deeply believe – is a message of mercy. We are all sinners, all in need of God's mercy. I believe that the majority of Christian conversions happen through one-on-one conversations (although unlike everything else I say in this book, I'm not giving a data-filled footnote to back that up). And so, I believe that our main goal is to always bring the person right in front us closer to God and to the truth.

The purpose of this (sometimes snarky) work is not to condemn those who support abortion, have had abortions, or even those who perform abortions. It is to expose a grave error in the hope that they themselves will be forced to confront the evil that plagues their lives *and* our nation.

On the off chance that those performing abortions don't read this book, the other purpose is to arm you, the reader, with the arguments and knowledge you need to take down our nation's greatest sin. *A la lucha.* To the fight.

Abortion and *Roe v. Wade* from a Lawyer's Easy-to-Understand Perspective. Did someone drop these judges on their heads when *they* were babies??

About the kindest thing you can say for the judges on the Supreme Court in 1973 is that someone must have dropped them on their heads when they were babies. Realistically, though, they wanted the Constitution to back their personal views, so they simply claimed that it did.

As a result of this, and for a very short time, legal doctrine in the United States moved unquestionably in the direction of strong protection for abortion. *Roe v. Wade* in 1973 was the high-water mark, and held that, throughout most of the pregnancy, unborn children are not persons, and so not protected under the law.

But, after *Roe*, constitutional protection for abortion began to be limited, not expanded. Before *Roe*, the tide of legal doctrine had only briefly been favorable to abortion rights, as the court pointed out in its own *Roe* ruling, making the *Roe* case little more than a legal island surrounded by controversy, and created by a rogue Supreme Court.

Legal lead-up.

Let's start from the beginning – the legal history of *Roe*. It is not hard to trace (even if it *doesn't* adhere to common sense).

Looking at the cases: the right to privacy as *Roe's* centerpiece.

The first cases we'll examine are those cases that the Supreme Court cited as the legal foundation for the so-called "right to privacy" which the court said "is broad enough to encompass a woman's decision whether or not to terminate her pregnancy."[1]

In other words, these cases and the "right to privacy" they created (out of nearly thin air) are the basis for the decision in *Roe*. The assumption that the Constitution includes a vague and broad "right to privacy" is the only thing that allowed the *Roe* court to declare abortion a protected right.

Yet before we even get to the cases, it's worth pointing out that the *Roe* court couldn't even make up its own mind on why the justices made the decision that they did. The court declined to even determine an exact basis for its own ruling, stating: "This right [to privacy]...[may] be founded in the Fourteenth Amendment's concept of personal liberty and restrictions upon state action...or...in the Ninth Amendment's reservation of rights to the people...."[2]

Partly as a result of its indecisiveness, the cases cited by the court present a wide variety of possibilities for where the right to privacy actually comes from. The following are the key cases the court cited (with explanations as to why the court's reliance on them doesn't make sense):

1. *Union Pac. R. Co. v. Botsford*: The first case the *Roe* court cited in defense of the right to privacy was *Union Pac. R. Co. v. Botsford*, a United States Supreme Court case.

    The case concerned whether a woman who had suffered injuries caused by the defendant (a railroad company) could be ordered by a court in a civil case "...without his or her consent, to submit to a surgical examination..."[3]

---

[1] *Roe v. Wade* 410 U.S. 113, 93 S.Ct. 705, 727 (1973).
[2] *Ibid*. Emphasis added.
[3] *Union Pac. R. Co. v. Botsford* 141 U.S. 250, 11 S.Ct. 1000, 1001 (1891)

In short, the railroad wanted the woman (Clara L. Botsford) to undergo a court-ordered examination to prove that her injuries were as extensive as she claimed. The Supreme Court, however, ruled that a court could *not* order her to undergo an examination. Rather, it would have to be voluntary.

The *Botsford* court did *not* mention a specific right to privacy, and so that language in *Roe* could not have come from the *Botsford* decision. Of greater concern, however (for any defenders of the *Roe* decision) is that this case involved whether or not a court could *order* someone to *have* a medical examination. Why is that a problem for the decision in *Roe*?

In *Roe*, the question was much different. Roe examined whether a state government (Texas) could *ban* a procedure it considered contrary to public morality and safety, and protect what it felt was a person (the child).

That's very different from deciding whether someone has the right to simply say *no* to a medical procedure that someone *else* wants them to have, in a situation involving no issue of a child's life, and concerning civil rather than criminal law.

At the risk of repeating myself (and deviating from discussing *Botsford*) the court in *Roe* said the government didn't have the *authority* to ban abortion, even if it caused risk to life. Yet, that would actually make the Supreme Court justices rather hypocritical when it comes to other issues.

Many states have used just such "banning" authority (referred to as negative authority) to ban a different procedure – physician assisted suicide – and the Supreme Court has declared such bans to be completely legal.[4]

If the court has to make either abortion or physician assisted suicide a protected right (I don't recommend either) shouldn't it legalize suicide first? After all, that technically concerns no life but that of the person making the decision. Yet somehow, the court feels that of the two, abortion is the one on which We The People shouldn't even be allowed to vote. Are they kidding?

The Food and Drug Administration (FDA) also uses negative authority to restrict what medicines are available on the open market - even though the use of experimental treatments solely affects the body of the person agreeing to take them. The Supreme Court has never suggested the FDA's work is illegal.

But where it is not someone's own body at risk, but the body of an unborn, helpless child that a state wishes to protect, the court in *Roe* confusingly decided to give much more "freedom."

2. *Terry v. Ohio*: Another case relied on by the justices in *Roe* is *Terry v. Ohio*. That case involved a police officer pat-down of someone the officer suspected of having a weapon. I'm sure that you, like the Supreme Court, immediately understand how important a case on police officer pat-downs is to abortion rights.[5] On second thought...maybe you don't. Neither do I, but I'll try to follow the court's logic.

---

[4] *Vacco v. Quill* 521 U.S. 793, 117 S.Ct. 2293. The Supreme Court declared bans on Physician Assisted Suicide to be legal.
[5] Yes, that would be sarcasm.

The Supreme Court in *Terry* confirmed that it *is* constitutional for a police officer to conduct a pat-down when someone is suspected of having a weapon.[6] But the court in *Terry* also noted that the "Fourth Amendment *does* provide...'the right of the people to be secure in their persons...'"[7]

This right to be "secure in their persons" was used by the *Roe* court as justification for the creation of a vague right to privacy, *and hence abortion.*

However, the very decision of the *Terry* case, in which a pat-down *was* allowed, supports the idea that a state may in fact invade the security of a person *in important public safety and health related causes.*

In short, if the people of, say, Pennsylvania, are concerned about someone's health or safety (such as that of a police officer or unborn baby) they can pass legislation to protect that person. They can allow a police officer to pat down a dangerous suspect. They can even tell a man and woman who decided to have sex[8] that they can't simply kill their child to resolve what may be a difficult set of circumstances.

Just as importantly, as in the *Botsford* case (discussed above) the *Terry* case involves what the government *can*

---

[6] *Terry v. Ohio* 392 U.S. 1, 88 S.Ct. 1868 (1968).

[7] *Terry v. Ohio* 392 U.S. 1, 88 S.Ct. 1868, 1873 (1968)

[8] Obviously, rape cases present a significant issue over whether abortion should be legal, because women in those cases were not given a chance to decide, and had a criminal act committed against them. However, that does not change the fact that the vast majority of pregnancies result from voluntary sex. Nor does it diminish the human life of a baby.

do, as opposed to what the government can *prevent* a citizen from doing (indeed, the *Terry* court cited the *Botsford* decision[9]). In other words, the *Terry* case doesn't show what the Roe court claims it does. The fact that a Police Officer *can* pat down a suspect he reasonably believes to be armed doesn't mean the government *cannot* significantly restrict abortion. That would make no sense.

3. *Meyer v. Nebraska*: The *Roe* court (as briefly discussed above) believed that the first part of the Fourteenth Amendment provides the best support for their supposed "right to privacy" – which in turn protects legalized abortion.

    To back their constitutional interpretation, the justices relied on a case called *Meyer v. Nebraska*. *Meyer* was a case in which the State of Nebraska attempted to ban the teaching of the German language to students, even if their parents wanted them to learn.[10] This was primarily a reaction to the fact that the United States had recently been at war with Germany (World War I). Nebraska wished to ensure that children were brought up as loyal Americans. The *Meyer* court ended up ruling that Nebraska could not impose such a ban.

    But in *Meyer*, the *Roe* court again cited a case which mentions no right to privacy.[11]

---

[9] *Ibid*.

[10] The state also banned the teaching of other foreign languages, although German was likely their primary concern.

[11] *Meyer v. Nebraska* 262 U.S. 390, 43 S.Ct. 625 (1973).

The opinion in *Meyer* is short, and the closest it comes to a right to privacy or to reproductive/abortive rights is to say that parents have the right to control their child's education. The *Meyer* court observes that "...the right[s] of parents...to instruct their children, we think, are within the liberty of the amendment."[12]

The court's recognition of the right of parents to educate children as the parents see fit is not, however, quite the same as recognizing the right to murder their children, born or unborn. To say the same thing in another way, *Meyer* deals with the right to raise children in the best way that parents know how, whereas *Roe* deals with the right not to raise them at all.

Thus, the court should have found no support for its *Roe* decision in the *Meyer* case.

4. *Griswold v. Connecticut*: The final case that is important for us to examine is *Griswold v. Connecticut*. The case concerned whether Connecticut could ban the sale of contraceptives. The Supreme Court ruled that the state could not, thus strictly limiting the government's role in the personal relationships of Americans.

Griswold is different from the three previous cases in that, if valid, it does in part support the ruling in *Roe* (and additionally, a right to privacy).

This is because, if *Griswold* is valid, the reproductive rights of each individual become, in the words of the *Griswold* court, a "sacred area" in which the state is normally forbidden from interfering[13] (since *Griswold* is a

---

[12] *Meyer v. Nebraska* 262 U.S. 390, 43 S.Ct. 625, 627 (1973).

contraception case, this includes the right *not* to reproduce). The *Griswold* decision also definitively states that there is, in fact, a right to privacy in the area of reproductive rights.[14]

Because of those things, *Griswold* is often seen as the most significant forerunner of *Roe*, even though the Supreme Court in *Roe* cited the most likely source for a right to privacy as coming from "the Fourteenth [Amendment]"[15] (not the Bill of Rights, on which the *Griswold* decision relies).

But that rather large flaw in the logic of relying on the *Griswold* decision isn't the most significant problem with the *Griswold* case for *Roe* defenders.

The biggest problem with *Roe* as it relates to *Griswold* is that *Griswold* was decided incorrectly in the first place. To be clear, this is not to say that Americans shouldn't have privacy when it comes to personal relationships. But *Griswold* didn't follow the constitution – or the law.

The *Roe* court cited *Griswold* for the proposition that the Constitutional right to privacy was to be found "in the penumbras [shadows] of the Bill of Rights"[16]. This is in reference to the fact that the *Griswold* opinion goes through a number of prior cases saying that they "suggest that specific guarantees in the Bill of Rights have penumbras [gray areas of extended legal protection], formed by things that go hand in hand with those guarantees that help give them life and substance."[17]

---

[13] *Griswold v. Connecticut* 381 U.S. 479, 85 S.Ct. 1678, 1682 (1965).
[14] *Ibid.*
[15] *Roe v. Wade* 410 U.S. 113, 93 S.Ct. 705, 727 (1973).
[16] *Ibid* at 726.

If you're already confused, I don't blame you. The murkier the legal language, the more likely it is that someone is trying to deceive you. Suffice it to say that the Court in *Griswold* meant that that Bill of Rights (such as the right to free speech/religion/bearing arms) doesn't mean much unless the Supreme Court implies other rights into it.

There's a tiny bit of truth in that. The right to *own* a firearm doesn't mean much if you don't have a right to *buy* one, for example. But that doesn't mean that any right, such as the right to an abortion, can be created out of the Bill of Rights by a creative judge. That would destroy the point of having a constitution.

However, let's accept, for the sake of argument, that "Various guarantees [in the Bill of Rights] create zones of privacy." (*Griswold*)[18] Those guarantees, according to the *Griswold* Court, include:

> "The right of association contained in the penumbra of the First Amendment is one, as we have seen. The Third Amendment in its prohibition against the quartering of soldiers 'in any house' in time of peace without the consent of the owner is another facet of that privacy. The Fourth Amendment explicitly affirms the 'right of the people to be secure in their persons, houses, papers, and effects, against unreasonable searches and seizures.' The Fifth Amendment in its Self-Incrimination Clause enables the citizen to create a zone of privacy which

---

[17] *Griswold v. Connecticut*, 381 U.S. 479, 85 S.Ct. 1678, 1681.
[18] *Ibid*.

government may not force him to surrender to his detriment. The Ninth Amendment provides: 'The enumeration in the Constitution, of certain rights, shall not be construed to deny or disparage others retained by the people.' "[19]

Beginning with the last of these, the Ninth Amendment cannot be construed to have a penumbra that is necessary to protect rights granted by that amendment, because no specific rights are granted by the Ninth Amendment. That amendment states "The enumeration in the Constitution of certain rights shall not be construed to deny or disparage others retained by the people."[20]

The concern inherent in the creation of the Ninth Amendment was that a bill of rights would been seen as a list of the *only* rights the American people had. This idea is fundamentally at odds with the concept that the Ninth *creates* any specific rights (let alone a right to avoid parenthood).

The concern of our nation's founding fathers that gave rise to the Ninth Amendment is in fact seen in *The Federalist Papers #84* [an essay in support of the Constitution] written by American founding father Alexander Hamilton:

> "I go further, and affirm that the bill of rights, in the sense and to the extent they are contended for, are not only un-necessary in the proposed constitution, but would even be dangerous. They would contain various exceptions to

---

[19] *Ibid.*
[20] The Constitution of the United States.

powers not granted [to the federal government]; and on this very account, would afford a colourable pretext to claim more than were granted. For why declare that things shall not be done, which there is no power to do?"[21]

What is more, the Ninth Amendment can and should be used to slap the *Roe* decision down. Remember, it provides that: "The enumeration in the Constitution, of certain rights, shall not be construed to deny or disparage others retained by the people."

Think about that. If we pretend, for just a moment, that it *is* possible to logically find a "right to abortion" in the constitution…it would still – oddly enough – be impossible to find such a right in the Constitution.

Why?

Well, let's think about it. If the *"enumeration in the constitution of certain rights"* cannot be construed to *"deny or disparage others retained by the people"* then the question is really…are the unborn *people*???[22] If they are, then the right of a woman to an abortion cannot *deny or disparage* the rights of the baby. Specifically, the Fifth Amendment's constitutional right not to "be deprived of life, liberty, or property, without due process of law."[23]

---

[21] Alexander Hamilton, "The Federalist 84" in The American Republic Primary Sources, ed. Bruce Frohnen (Indianapolis: Liberty Fund, Inc., 2002), pp. 301, 302. Section inside brackets added for clarity.
[22] Using Abraham Lincoln's arguments concerning slavery, I prove (below) why babies *must* be thought of as people.
[23] U.S. Constitution. The Bill of Rights: A Transcription. United States National Archives. https://www.archives.gov/founding-docs/bill-of-rights-transcript (Accessed November 30th, 2018).

Did I miss the part where babies were given a jury trial before being aborted?

In fact, even if one gave them a jury trial, and they were duly convicted of inconveniencing their mothers, or even of causing any harm short of likely death to *both* mother and child, they could not be executed by either the government or their parents. This is because the Supreme Court has specifically ruled that no crime short of murder can be punished with execution. According to the court's decision in *Kennedy v. Louisiana*, not even a defendant convicted of *the rape of an eight-year old* can be executed, unless the rape is combined with a killing (homicide).[24]

But let's move on from the Ninth Amendment.

As seen above, the court also cites several other sections of the Bill of Rights as creating a protective zone of privacy. None of these make much sense when used in support of the right to contraception in *Griswold* that the *Roe* court used to force the legalization of abortion.

It is hard to imagine, to begin with, that the Constitution's framers (creators) had contraception in mind (it did exist at the time) when they created the rights mentioned in *Griswold*.

Does the right to free speech automatically create a right to contraception or abortion?

---

[24] *Kennedy v. Louisiana*, 554 U.S. 407. I vehemently disagree with the 2008 decision in *Kennedy*, concerning whether a man who raped an eight-year old can be executed. The idea that raping a child cannot ruin the child's life as effectively as murdering them is not only absurd, but ignores the fact that America's founding generation *did* execute rapists, and saw no need for a constitutional provision to prevent such executions.

What about the right not to have soldiers quartered in your home – does that (as the *Roe* court believed) create the right to an abortion or contraception?[25]

What about the Constitution's protection against warrantless searches and seizures? Or the Fifth Amendment right against self-incrimination?

All of these rights are wonderful, but it is hard to imagine the constitution's framers wanted to protect abortion when they created a right not to have soldiers forcibly take over someone's house. In fact, one of the most *liberal* justices on the Supreme Court pointed this out. In his dissent to the *Griswold* majority opinion, Justice Black said:

> "[T]he law [banning contraception] is every bit as offensive to me as it is my Brethren of the majority and my Brothers HARLAN, WHITE and GOLDBERG who, reciting reasons why it is offensive to them, hold it unconstitutional. There is no single one of the graphic and eloquent strictures and criticisms fired at the policy of this Connecticut law either by the Court's opinion or by those of my concurring Brethren to which I cannot subscribe-except their conclusion that the evil qualities they see in the law make it unconstitutional."[26]

---

[25] While some moms going through difficult pregnancies might feel like they have a crazy soldier quartered in their womb, I don't think that was what the Constitution was referring to.

[26] *Griswold v. Connecticut*, 381 U.S. 479, 85 S.Ct. 1678, 1694.

Translation: Just because you feel your rights have been violated doesn't mean the Constitution agrees with you.

Further, even assuming that these or other constitutional rights support a right to use contraception, it is harder to argue that the same logic would also support the kind of right to privacy needed to back the *Roe* decision.

The First Amendment, for example, does create a right to free association. For the sake of argument, let's assume that that right includes anything happening under the auspices of an intimate relationship. Would *that* cover abortion, making it unconstitutional for states to ban it?

To quote St. Paul – "no."[27] (I'm sure he said 'no' at some point – in his case to a fair number of things!).

Abortion is not about being able to associate with another freely; it is about being able to avoid the consequence of that association. Saying that those who engage in intimate acts may pass the consequences of those actions to the unborn is like saying that not only does someone have the right to free speech, but that no one else is allowed to be upset with what they say.

Granted, in our politically-correct culture, lots of liberals think that no one *should* be able to criticize what they say, especially concerning feminism, race, and a host of other topics including abortion – but I digress.

Liberals may want to free everyone from personal responsibility, but the Constitution was, if anything, designed to do the opposite – to give the most freedom (and thus responsibility) possible. A respect for virtue, truth, and basic human decency are central to that. As our second president John Adams stated, "Liberty can no

---

[27] St. Paul.

more exist without virtue and independence, than the body can live and move without a soul."

In restricting abortion, a state government is in no way restricting physical intimacy or the freedom to express oneself. Nor is it violating the right not to have soldiers quartered in one's home, the right not to self-incriminate, or deciding it can rifle through someone's papers. It is only saying that it will not allow doctors within the state's borders to murder innocent babies, or violate the medical tradition of "do no harm".

So much for *Roe's* arguments based on *Griswold*.

Thus ends our examination of the cases cited by the Supreme Court in support of *Roe*. Now on to abortion's legal decline.

Legal Decline of Abortion – Retreat from the High-Water Mark

The Supreme Court's protection of abortion rights, having reached its high point with *Roe* in 1973, was in decline within nineteen years. For the court, this time period was amazingly short. The court's infamous *Plessy v. Ferguson* decision (allowing race-based separate but "equal" facilities)[28] took place in 1896, and it was fifty-eight years before the court reconsidered it in *Brown v. Board of Education* in 1954.[29]

Two key court cases are discussed below, each of which show how *Roe* has now been limited by subsequent decisions. In fact, it could be argued that the first of these two cases effectively overturns *Roe*. Both cases show the Supreme Court tacking in the direction of recognizing the personhood of the unborn. Both

---

[28] *Plessy v. Ferguson* 163 U.S. 537, 16 S.Ct. 1896.
[29] *Brown v. Board of Ed. of Topeka, Shawnee County, Kan.* 347 U.S. 483, 74 S.Ct. 686 (1954).

cases also put power back into the hands of the citizens of individual states.

1. *Planned Parenthood v. Casey* (1992): The first case we'll discuss demonstrates the Court backtracking, not just to recognize the personhood of unborn children, but also to recognize a state government's right to interfere in abortion at an earlier stage in the pregnancy than the *Roe* court would have, and in doing both, destroying *Roe's* underlying logic. That case is the *Planned Parenthood v. Casey*.

The *Casey* decision begins by claiming to uphold *Roe*, saying: "we are led to conclude this: the essential holding *of Roe v. Wade* should be retained..."[30] Yet the *Casey* court did not leave *Roe* "essentially" intact.

The *Roe* court had decided what it felt was the proper time at which a state would be enabled to interfere with a woman's "right" to an abortion, thus: "With respect to the State's important...interest in the health of the mother [note that the *Roe* court wasn't even considering the life of the child here] the 'compelling' point, in the light of present medical knowledge, is at approximately the end of the first trimester."[31] The court continued: "This is so because of the now-established medical fact...that until the end of the first trimester mortality in abortion may be less than...in normal childbirth."[32]

In other words, the *Roe* court would allow no interference with abortion during the first trimester.

---

[30] *Planned Parenthood of Southeastern Pennsylvania v. Casey*, 505 U.S. 833, 112 S.Ct. 2791, 2804 (1992).
[31] *Roe v. Wade* 410 U.S. 113, 93 S.Ct. 705, 731 (1973).
[32] *Ibid.*

18

However, *Casey* overrules this, stating; "a necessary reconciliation of the liberty of the woman and the interest of the State in promoting prenatal life, require, in our view, that we abandon the trimester framework..."[33] In saying this [abandoning the trimester system] the *Casey* court recognized that medical advances had changed the court's view of prenatal life; "We have seen how time has overtaken some of Roe's factual assumptions... advances in neonatal care have advanced viability to a point somewhat earlier."[34]

Thus, in one stroke, the court acknowledges changed assumptions about human life due to medical advances, and sets a new standard for a state's compelling interest in the unborn life. It essentially says that (1) the state always has some interest in human life and (2) that the interest becomes especially important once the baby reaches the point of *viability* (the ability of the baby to survive outside of the womb).

The problem for pro-abortion advocates is that this new standard is likely to continue pushing a state's 'compelling state interest in prenatal life' closer and closer to the point of conception. This is because, according to the court itself, viability, and thus the point at which states can regulate abortion, will be pushed ever to earlier points in the pregnancy by the inevitable advance of medical science.

In other words, on the day a baby can survive outside the womb, with or without medical intervention, abortion of that baby is something states can highly regulate, or even ban. Thus, according to the court, the point at which we can protect the life of the baby is; "twenty-eight weeks, as was

[33] *Planned Parenthood of Southeastern Pennsylvania v. Casey*, 505 U.S. 833, 112 S.Ct. 2791, 2817 (1992).
[34] *Planned Parenthood of Southeastern Pennsylvania v. Casey*, 505 U.S. 833, 112 S.Ct. 2791, 2811 (1992).

usual at the time of Roe...**twenty-three to twenty-four weeks**,[35] as it sometimes [is] today, or at some moment even slightly earlier in pregnancy, as [the point of viability] may [be] if fetal respiratory capacity can somehow be enhanced in the future."[36]

But the *Casey* court goes further than merely acknowledging a new ever-changing scale for abortion rights based purely on medical advances. It essentially states that it is overruling the trimester framework *because it was wrong from the start*. In doing so, it clearly overrules *Roe*, even though the *Casey* court (as already noted) denies it is doing so. This is the key passage from the *Casey* decision:

> "The trimester framework, however, does not fulfill Roe's own promise that the State has an interest in protecting fetal life or potential life. Roe began the contradiction by using the trimester framework to forbid any regulation of abortion designed to advance that interest before viability...Before viability, Roe and subsequent cases treat all governmental attempts to influence a woman's decision on behalf of the potential life within her as unwarranted. This treatment is, in our judgment, incompatible with the recognition that ***there is a substantial state interest in potential life throughout pregnancy***."[37] [38]

---

[35] My emphasis.

[36] *Ibid*, contents of brackets and emphasis are mine.

[37] *Planned Parenthood of Southeastern Pennsylvania v. Casey*, 505 U.S. 833, 112 S.Ct. 2791, 2820 (1992).

[38] My emphasis.

The court continues this line of logic by ruling; "We also see no reason why the State may not require doctors to inform a woman seeking an abortion of the availability of materials relating to the consequences to the fetus, even when those consequences have no direct relation to her health."[39]

This is, by itself, a large step in the direction of acknowledging the personhood of the unborn child (or perhaps it even does tacitly recognize it) and, just as importantly, the right of states to recognize it.

In fact, the very next sentence of *Casey* does provide such a recognition of fetal personhood, though the court does not acknowledge it, thus; "An example illustrates the point. We would think it constitutional for the State to require that in order for there to be informed consent to a kidney transplant operation the recipient must be supplied with information about risks to the donor as well as risks to himself or herself."[40]

At a first glance, this sentence may not seem to have large consequences. But look again at the comparison the court is drawing here. It is between informing someone about to receive a transplant of the danger to the donor, versus informing the mother of a danger to the unborn child.

Now, why would an individual want to know about the danger to their organ donor? They would want to know because that donor is not merely human tissue, but a person. Since the court is comparing that situation to an abortion, the natural conclusion is that the court acknowledges that a state has the right to recognize an unborn child as a human person. If not, then the court's comparison (between an

---

[39] *Planned Parenthood of Southeastern Pennsylvania v. Casey*, 505 U.S. 833, 112 S.Ct. 2791, 2823 (1992).
[40] *Ibid*.

adult organ donor and an unborn child) would make no sense.

So, the court in *Casey* effectively overruled the court in *Roe* on many of *Roe's* key points. *Casey* took a very long step in the direction of recognizing the rights of states to prevent most abortions, and certainly recognized a compelling state interest in fetal life at least four weeks earlier than *Roe* did (24 vs. 28, as noted above) due to advances in medical understanding. In addition, *Casey* acknowledged as a legal standard that "there is a substantial state interest in potential life throughout pregnancy."[41]

2. *Gonzales v. Carhart*: The second key Supreme Court case we look at here also shows the Supreme Court moving closer to allowing state recognition of personhood for the unborn. That case is *Gonzales v. Carhart*. While not quite as damaging to *Roe* as *Casey*, it is still an important case to consider.

   Essentially, *Gonzales v. Carhart* concerns whether the federal government could ban entirely a certain *kind* of abortion procedure, thought to be especially barbaric toward the unborn child (specifically, partial birth abortion).[42] The court answered in the affirmative. In doing so, it then added a number of key points (below) showing great respect for unborn life.

   As with *Casey*, this case tends toward recognizing the life in the womb as something significantly more than mere tissue – at least if the court were to allow its logic to flow to its

---

[41] *Planned Parenthood of Southeastern Pennsylvania v. Casey*, 505 U.S. 833, 112 S.Ct. 2791, 2820 (1992).
[42] *Gonzales v. Carhart*, 550 U.S. 124, 127 S.Ct. 1610 (2007).

ultimate conclusion. Here are some of the key aspects of the decision:

- The court makes a specific point of accepting the language of the law being challenged in *Carhart*, stating; "Implicitly approving such a brutal and inhumane procedure...will further coarsen society to the humanity not only of newborns, but all...innocent human life..."[43]
- The court stated; "The government may use its voice and its regulatory authority to show its profound respect for the life within the woman."[44]
- And last but not least, the court opined; "Respect for human life finds an ultimate expression in the bond of love the mother has for her child" and "some women come to regret their choice to abort the infant life they once created and sustained."[45]

That certainly doesn't sound like a court that has much use for the killing of unborn children.

In conclusion, there is now a revived and growing legal trend at the Supreme Court level toward supporting the idea that a state can pass laws recognizing personhood in the unborn. There is also a growing trend on the high court toward doing away with the legal logic underpinning *Roe v. Wade*. Conservatives can help bring this new movement to its fulfillment. Especially with help from all who respect life.

---

[43] *Gonzales v. Carhart*, 550 U.S. 124, 127 S.Ct. 1610, 1633 (2007). Emphasis Added.
[44] *Ibid*.
[45] *Gonzales v. Carhart*, 550 U.S. 124, 127 S.Ct. 1610, 1634 (2007). Emphasis Added.

Here is some additional case law on the subject of abortion, for those who are most interested in the legal aspects of abortion, or simply want to read more about that topic:

1. *Mazurek v. Armstrong* (1997) – A legislative body may pass a law stating that only doctors may perform an abortion, and not (for example) a physician assistant or nurse.

2. *Rust v. Sullivan* (1991) – The Government may make a value judgment favoring childbirth over abortion and implement that judgment by the allocation of public funds.

3.

How Abortion Affects Minorities and Women

How abortion affects Blacks and Hispanics

According to the United States Government's Center for Disease Control and Prevention (CDC) in 2012, 36.7 percent of abortions in the United States were performed on black women.[46] By contrast, according to the United States Census Bureau, only about 13.3 percent of the American population was primarily black as of 2016.[47] That means that in 2012, black children were aborted at a rate of more than 2.8 times that of the general population.

Sometimes, though, in America, we get bombarded by these kind statistics to the point where they don't really sink in. "Unemployment is at 4 percent!", says a sitting president. "No, 10 percent!", screams the opposition party. Pretty soon, those in politics notice that they can combat the statistics of others by simply making up their own, or brushing the facts off entirely.

The left knows that, and they use it. Although we don't know for certain if he said this (see, I'm honest with you when I'm not sure about something!) Communist Dictator Joseph Stalin is often quoted as saying; "One death is a tragedy – one million is a statistic."

---

[46] Pazol, Karen, PhD, Andreea A. Creanga, MD, PhD, Denise J Jamieson, MD. "Abortion Surveillance — United States, 2012." Published 2015. CDC.gov.
https://www.cdc.gov/mmwr/preview/mmwrhtml/ss6410a1.htm?s_cid=ss6410a1_e (accessed November 29, 2018).
[47] United States Census Bureau. "Quick Facts United States." Published 2018. CENSUS.gov
https://www.census.gov/quickfacts/fact/table/US/PST045216 (accessed December 15, 2018).

That sums up the attitude of the left nicely. Ask them to defend abortion, and they don't give you numbers, they give you stories. You'll never hear from them just how much abortion affects blacks, and the statistics are so mind-boggling that most people never really delve into them. But the left will always tell you about "that one time when abortion saved the life of a mother."

So...in order to cut through the "statistical noise" here, we have to ask ourselves a question. And that is - what do those abortion numbers mean for African Americans in real terms? What if we were to count every death by abortion as if it were...a death?

According to a group of researchers at the University of North Carolina, that would mean that abortion accounts for over 61% of all deaths in the black community.[48] [49]

Now THAT's attention grabbing.

Even half that number of deaths would never be considered acceptable if the cause of death were cancer or a heart-attack.[50] If we saw abortion deaths the way we see cancer deaths, we would have fundraising marches "for the cure" (for life, in this case) in every major town. Baseball games dedicated

---

[48] Studnicki, James, Sharon J. MacKinnon, John W. Fisher. "Induced Abortion, Mortality, and the Conduct of Science." Published 2016. SCIRP.org. http://www.scirp.org/journal/PaperInformation.aspx?paperID=67433 (accessed August 3, 2018).
[49] Stark, Paul. "Researchers Find Abortion is the Leading Cause of Death, Surpassing Heart Disease and Cancer." Published 2018. LIFENEWS.COM. http://www.lifenews.com/2018/08/02/researchers-find-abortion-is-the-leading-cause-of-death-surpassing-heart-disease-and-cancer/ (Accessed August 4, 2018).
[50] Or deaths resulting from police encounters.

to ending abortion, t-shirts in a highly recognizable color to memorialize the babies we lost. But we don't.

Data from some of the same organizations tells a similar, though slightly less dramatic story when it comes to Americans of Hispanic descent. Although the percentage of U.S. abortions that occur among Hispanic women[51] is only about 1% higher than the Hispanic percentage of overall population,[52] it is dramatically different from the white abortion rate.

For example, the abortion rate among white women in 2012 was about 7.7 abortions for every 1,000 women, whereas the Hispanic abortion rate was 15.3 abortions for every 1,000 women – making the abortion rate among Hispanics almost twice as high.[53]

But for Hispanics, that's not the whole story.

The CDC states that 699,202 abortions were reported in the United States in 2012.[54] This does not, however, include all abortions, since the most populous state in the nation, California, did not even report its abortion statistics. Neither did Florida, Maryland, New Hampshire, or Washington DC.

---

[51] Pazol, Karen, PhD, Andreea A. Creanga, MD, PhD, Denise J Jamieson, MD. "Abortion Surveillance — United States, 2012." Published 2015. CDC.gov. https://www.cdc.gov/mmwr/preview/mmwrhtml/ss6410a1.htm?s_cid=ss6410a1_e (accessed November 29, 2018).
[52] United States Census Bureau. "Quick Facts United States." Published 2018. CENSUS.gov https://www.census.gov/quickfacts/fact/table/US/PST045216 (accessed December 15, 2018).
[53] Pazol, Karen, PhD, Andreea A. Creanga, MD, PhD, Denise J Jamieson, MD. "Abortion Surveillance — United States, 2012." Published 2015. CDC.gov. https://www.cdc.gov/mmwr/preview/mmwrhtml/ss6410a1.htm?s_cid=ss6410a1_e (accessed November 29, 2018).
[54] *Ibid.*

Those states alone, plus Washington D.C., make up at least 20 percent of the U.S. population. And California – America's most populous state – has the nation's largest Hispanic population.[55] In fact, Hispanics make up at least 40 percent of the people there, and are the largest racial/ethnic group. This means that abortions done in California are likely to have an even greater demographic impact on Hispanics than in other states.

In 2014, the well-respected Guttmacher Institute reported that there was actually a total of about 926,200 abortions in the United States,[56] whereas only about 652,639 were reported to the CDC the same year.[57] Given the number and size of the states that didn't even report to the CDC, it is likely that the Guttmacher Institute's numbers are closer to reality.

That being the case, and given that Hispanic women account for about 18% of all abortion recipients according to the CDC,[58] about 160,000 Hispanic babies likely died in 2012 alone as

[55] Stepler, Renee, Mark Hugo Lopez. "Ranking the Latino population in the states." Published 2016. PEWHISPANIC.ORG. http://www.pewhispanic.org/2016/09/08/4-ranking-the-latino-population-in-the-states/ (accessed December 2, 2018).
[56] Jones, Rachel K., Jerman, Jenna "Abortion Incidence and Service Availability In the United States, 2014." Published 2017. GUTTMACHER.org https://www.guttmacher.org/journals/psrh/2017/01/abortion-incidence-and-service-availability-united-states-2014 (accessed December 6, 2018).
[57]Jatlaoui. Tara C., Md., Jill Shah, MPH, Michele G. Mandel, etc. "Abortion Surveillance — United States, 2014." Published 2017. CDC.gov. https://www.cdc.gov/mmwr/volumes/66/ss/ss6624a1.htm (Accessed December 6, 2018).
[58] Pazol, Karen, PhD, Andreea A. Creanga, MD, PhD, Denise J Jamieson, MD. "Abortion Surveillance — United States, 2012." Published 2015. CDC.gov. https://www.cdc.gov/mmwr/preview/mmwrhtml/ss6410a1.htm?s_cid=ss6410a1_e (accessed November 29, 2018).

a result abortion. That 160,000 number really puts the CDC's "15.3 abortions for every 1,000 [Hispanic] women" into perspective.

Since abortion-loving leftists and Democrats are so eager to increase the Hispanic population via immigration, maybe they ought to try ending abortion first.

But liberals won't do that. Most of their leaders care about people of other backgrounds only in the abstract. They care about Muslims, women, and high-school students in danger from mass-shootings only so long as it involves nothing more than a sign-waving protest march where their followers can leave behind massive amounts of litter,[59] and they can get brownie points for being "socially aware/woke".

Flush with donation cash from the gullible, liberal leaders then get to keep their high-paying jobs running social-justice organizations. Or just use their awareness of, or participation in, the social-justice movement to sell products. We're looking at you, Pepsi.[60]

They ignore the way women and children in Muslim countries are treated. They care about blacks so much that they insist that public schools are wonderful, so long as rich liberals

---

[59] Zanotti, Emily. "GROSS: March For Our Lives Left A Lot Of Trash In Washington." Published 2018. DAILYWIRE.com. https://www.dailywire.com/news/28680/gross-march-our-lives-left-lot-trash-washington-emily-zanotti (accessed December 6, 2018).

[60] "Full Pepsi Commercial Starring Kendal Jenner" YouTube video, 2:48, posted by "Yash Yadav," April 6, 2017. Commercial originally aired in 2017. https://www.youtube.com/watch?v=uwvAgDCOdU4 (accessed September 1, 2018). Although the ad tried to promote Pepsi by latching on to and even supporting the popularity of leftist protests, the insane left criticized it anyway, saying it trivialized the issues involved in recent protests. I'm surprised we didn't get a protest march over the ad as well.

can send their kids to private schools where their children will never *actually* mix with poor inner-city African Americans.[61] And they care about Hispanics – as long as they're illegally crossing the border to take (for an even lower wage!) the job of the Hispanic person mowing the lawn of a rich Hollywood liberal (if you've ever lived in Southern California, as I did for three years, you'll know exactly what I mean).

Meanwhile, 79% of abortion clinics are within walking distance of a black or Hispanic neighborhood,[62] and according to famed black neurosurgeon Dr. Benjamin Carson (currently the United States Secretary of Housing and Urban Development) this is done specifically to control the minority population, in accordance with Planned Parenthood's racist history.[63]

"But that's crazy" you might say. Planned Parenthood isn't performing abortions out of a sense of racial superiority, right? That can't be!

If you're skeptical about Planned Parenthood's racist roots, here are two quotes from its founder, Margaret Sanger, according to the Washington Times:

---

[61] Burke, Lindsey. "How Members of the 111th Congress Practice Private School Choice." Published 2009. HERITAGE.org. https://www.heritage.org/education/report/how-members-the-111th-congress-practice-private-school-choice (accessed December 7, 2018).

[62] Ertelt, Steven. "79% of Planned Parenthood Abortion Clinics Target Blacks, Hispanics." Published 2012. LIFENEWS.com http://www.lifenews.com/2012/10/16/79-of-planned-parenthood-abortion-clinics-target-blacks-hispanics/ (accessed December 8, 2018).

[63] Hudson, Jerome. "Proof Ben Carson Is Right About Planned Parenthood Targeting Black Neighborhoods." Published 2015. BREITBART.com. http://www.breitbart.com/big-government/2015/08/13/proof-ben-carson-is-right-about-planned-parenthood-targeting-black-neighborhoods/ (accessed December 9, 2018).

"We do not want word to go out that we want to exterminate the Negro population, and the minister is the man who can straighten out that idea if it ever occurs to any of their more rebellious members"[64]

And:

"I accepted an invitation to talk to the women's branch of the Ku Klux Klan ... I saw through the door dim figures parading with banners and illuminated crosses ... I was escorted to the platform, was introduced, and began to speak ... In the end, through simple illustrations I believed I had accomplished my purpose. A dozen invitations to speak to similar groups were proffered".[65]

Isn't Margaret Sanger just a peach, ladies and gentlemen? If peaches were poisonous and covered in razor-wire, that is.

Now of course, I can't speak to the personal motivations of those currently running Planned Parenthood, but whether they realize it or not, their work has a racist end-game.

Need more evidence?

Racism isn't just the legacy of Planned Parenthood. It's the legacy of the Democratic Party that supports Planned Parenthood. Even President Barack Obama had this to say about the legacy of Democratic President Lyndon B. Johnson (the guy Democrats point to as their "turning point" on racism – the point

[64] Grossu, Arina. "Margaret Sanger, racist eugenicist extraordinaire." Published 2014. WASHINGTONTIMES.com. https://www.washingtontimes.com/news/2014/may/5/grossu-margaret-sanger-eugenicist/ (accessed December 9, 2018).
[65] Ibid.

at which the "party of the Confederacy" suddenly stopped supporting racist ideas): "During his first 20 years in Congress, Lyndon Johnson opposed every civil rights bill that came up for a vote, once calling the push for federal legislation a farce and a shame."[66]

Oddly enough, until at least the early 1960s, even Planned Parenthood, while advocating for contraception (especially in minority communities) was technically against abortion.[67] They are now America's largest abortion provider.

How Abortion Affects People With Disabilities

Most of us don't feel disgust when seeing a disabled person. We also don't assume that they have nothing of value to contribute to society, or to teach us. We certainly don't despise them as a burden.

The Nazis (Germany's socialist party from the 1920s to the 1940s) felt disgusted by the disabled however. According to the United States Holocaust Museum, they murdered thousands of mentally ill and disabled children,[68] and countless adults with similar problems. They also sterilized many of the mentally ill and

[66] Selby, W. Gardner. "Lyndon Johnson opposed every civil rights proposal considered in his first 20 years as lawmaker." Published 2014. POLITIFACT.com. http://www.politifact.com/texas/statements/2014/apr/14/barack-obama/lyndon-johnson-opposed-every-civil-rights-proposal/ (accessed December 9, 2018).
[67] "The Hippocratic Oath and Abortion." Eternity Matters. Published 2011. 1ETERNITYMATTERS.WORDPRES.COM. https://1eternitymatters.wordpress.com/2011/05/18/the-hippocratic-oath-and-abortion/ (accessed December 9, 2018).
[68] "Nazi Persecution of the Disabled: Murder of the "Unfit."" United States Holocaust Memorial Museum. USHMM.org. https://www.ushmm.org/information/exhibitions/online-exhibitions/special-focus/nazi-persecution-of-the-disabled (accessed December 11, 2018).

disabled. This was done to (supposedly) create a society free of genetically-based mental and physical problems.[69] Unfortunately, modern abortionists have the same goals.

Down Syndrome

Today, the United States "avoids" about 67%[70] of adult Down Syndrome cases, with the country of Iceland "leading the world" by avoiding about 80% (or more) of adult cases.[71]

Has a cure from Down Syndrome been found? That would certainly be great news. But as you have likely guessed, Down Syndrome cases have dropped for one reason only. As *CBS News* reported in 2017, babies at high risk of Down Syndrome are simply being murdered in the womb.[72]

With modern technology, women are usually given ultrasounds and other pre-birth tests that allow doctors to determine (although with far from perfect accuracy) what a particular child's risk for Down Syndrome might be. When Down Syndrome is detected, women are often advised to abort, thus leading to lower Down Syndrome rates in wealthy countries with more access to advanced medical technology.

This "solution" to Down Syndrome is like a doctor telling you he cured your mother of cancer, and when you ask him how he did it, he tells you that he shot her, and hands you her ashes in a jar (the Nazis basically did just that to families of individuals who had been at mental institutions being "treated"[73]).

---

[69] *Ibid.*

[70] Quinones, Julian. Arijeta Lajka. ""What kind of society do you want to live in?": Inside the country where Down syndrome is disappearing." Published 2017. CBSNEWS.COM. https://www.cbsnews.com/news/down-syndrome-iceland/ (accessed December 9, 2018).

[71] *Ibid.*

[72] *Ibid.*

Actually, check that. That's not "like" what this "solution" to Down Syndrome is. That's exactly what it is…murder.

In typical fashion, liberals and Democrats are utterly hypocritical about this.

For example, the ultra-liberal *Huffington Post* wrote in 2017 about how we should celebrate World Down Syndrome Day, comparing the issues of those with Down Syndrome to racism (Democrats compare everything to racism, despite having been the party of the South for the entire history of slavery and Jim Crow since 1828, when the party was founded).

In this case though, the comparison is an apt one – babies with Down Syndrome do deserve to be treated as more than just the "property" of the woman deciding she doesn't want them. And if a mentally ill person has to be in a place where they can receive a higher level of care than their families can provide, that place should be a genuinely caring and nurturing one that maximizes their potential.

But the *Huffington Post* is, in fact, a leading cheerleader for abortion – the number one killer of people with Down Syndrome. A quick search of their site reveals countless pro-abortion articles,[74] and virtually none with a pro-life slant.

Other leftist/Democrat supporting news sources are much the same, with *ABC News*,[75] the *New York Times*,[76] and *NBC*

---

[73] "Nazi Persecution of the Disabled: Murder of the "Unfit."" United States Holocaust Memorial Museum. USHMM.org. https://www.ushmm.org/information/exhibitions/online-exhibitions/special-focus/nazi-persecution-of-the-disabled (accessed December 11, 2018).
[74] Huffington Post. HUFFINGTONPOST.COM. https://www.huffingtonpost.com/topic/abortion (accessed December 21, 2018).
[75] Becker, Amy Julia. "On World Down Syndrome Day, a mother's tribute to her daughter's 'exceptional' community." Published 2018.

News[77] all having celebrated Down Syndrome awareness while offering rabid support for the Democrats who fight tooth and nail to keep abortion legal.

And if you don't think media bias in favor of Democrats is a real thing, consider this. According to the *ABC News* website: "George Stephanopoulos is ABC News' Chief Anchor. He also serves as anchor of "Good Morning America," and anchor of "This Week with George Stephanopoulos." As Chief Anchor, Stephanopoulos leads the network's coverage on all major live events and breaking news around the world."

George Stephanopoulos was once the *de facto* press secretary for Democratic President Bill Clinton, and helped to lead Clinton's 1992 presidential campaign. He later gave what I'm sure was totally unbiased coverage of Hillary Clinton's two presidential election campaigns to the twenty-million or so people who watch ABCs nightly news programs every single day.

Babies with Down Syndrome are Not the Only Ones at Risk

But enough with the media.

The fact is that people with Down Syndrome are not the only disabled individuals at risk due to abortion.

For example, 68% of babies with Spina Bifida are aborted[78] – despite the fact that Spina Bifida does not necessarily mean

ABCNEWS.GO.com. https://abcnews.go.com/GMA/Family/world-syndrome-day-mothers-tribute-daughters-exceptional-community/story?id=53900315 (accessed December 10, 2018).
[76] Collins, Glen. "Down's Syndrome and Sibling Love." Published 1981. NYTIMES.com. https://www.nytimes.com/1981/11/19/garden/down-s-syndrome-and-sibling-love.html (accessed December 11, 2018).
[77] "Meet the first Gerber baby with Down Syndrome." Published 2018. NBCNEWS.com. https://www.nbcnews.com/nightly-news/video/meet-the-first-gerber-baby-with-down-syndrome-1156218947600 (accessed December 11, 2018).

that a child will be mentally impaired. In fact, doctors can now perform incredible operations before a child is even born that can allow a child to grow up with no significant problems – operations where doctors literally remove the uterus, operate on it/the baby to fix the problem, and then put it (the uterus) back inside the woman so that the baby can finish developing.[79]

As with Down Syndrome, the excuse given for all these Spina Bifida abortions is simple – that it is really in the best interests of the child, who would suffer otherwise. Of course, all humans suffer, and I'd personally prefer my mother not shoot me when I'm feeling depressed. But that's just me.

In 2011, an article in the U.K.'s *The Daily Mail* (or as my favorite YouTube star refers to it, *The Daily Fail*) glorified a woman's supposedly brave and well-thought-out choice to abort her Spina Bifida positive child – even though there was a chance the child would be born with zero mental impairment.[80]

She was so far along in the pregnancy when the abortion took place that she had to allow the baby to be born in order to abort it (yes, the UK allowed her to murder a newborn – this one is for all the liberals out there who assured us that abortion would never turn into the murder of actual newborns).[81] During the process, she describes feeling like she was murdering her

---

[78] Andrusko, Dave. "Pennsylvania mother turns down abortion, chooses fetal surgery for unborn baby diagnosed with severe spina bifida." Published 2018. NATIONALRIGHTTOLIFENEWS.org https://www.nationalrighttolifenews.org/news/2018/02/pennsylvania-mother-turns-abortion-chooses-fetal-surgery-unborn-baby-diagnosed-severe-spina-bifida/ (accessed December 11, 2018).
[79] *Ibid.*
[80] Carpenter, Sara. "I saw my son's bleak future and knew I had to abort him." Published 2011. DAILYMAIL.CO.uk. http://www.dailymail.co.uk/femail/article-1388475/Abortion-baby-born-disability-What-choice-make.html (accessed December 11, 2018).
[81] *Ibid.*

child (because she was) and not wanting to go through with it (Hint for future mothers – don't go through with it. Walk away!).

She then admits feeling years of guilt, only assuaged by bringing another (this time fully healthy) child into the world (perhaps liberal leaders want to stick a knife in *that* child's back, if the child ever becomes disabled). The truly sad thing is that she probably really believed the liberal lie that she was doing the right thing, or at least convinced herself of it after deciding she didn't want to raise the child. And it took her a while to recover.

The healing process the woman is living/reciting is, in fact, what would normally be seen as the Christian process of seeking forgiveness (minus being actually sorry). Thus:

1. She feels guilty.
2. She confesses her sins in her article (she wrote the *Daily Mail* article herself).
3. She does penance/seeks atonement by bringing another baby into the world and caring for that baby, thus trying to make amends for not caring for the first.

However, I suspect she will continue to feel depressed until she realizes that what she did was actually wrong, and deals with the guilt.

Of course, concerning her attempt to make amends, Christians believe that only the mercy of Jesus can wash away our sins, and that no human act can substitute for His saving grace. But that's already been elaborated on by a much better author in another book.[82]

---

[82] I like to call that book "The Bible."

Incidentally, her need to make up for the previous pregnancy is essentially a tacit admission that the abortion was a mistake.

As a final note on Spina Bifida, Hispanic women are almost 19% more likely to conceive children with that condition than white women, according to the United States Government's CDC[83] – meaning that once again, abortion by the numbers is just a liberal campaign against minorities.

In addition to Down Syndrome and Spina Bifida, several other disabilities can get a child murdered in-utero. They include:[84] [85]

1. Having a cleft palate (eminently fixable via a simple surgery)
2. Deformed feet (not a huge barrier to happy life) and,
3. Cystic Fibrosis.

In the case of Cystic Fibrosis, while many who suffer from it may not live beyond their 30s and 40s, the vast majority of those who live to be at least 18 end up graduating from both high-school *and* college. Over one-third end up in long-term romantic relationships and/or get married. And given that just 60 years ago, most of those who suffered from Cystic Fibrosis died as infants, it is reasonable to believe that medical

[83] Centers for Disease Control and Prevention. "Data & Statistics on Spina Bifida." Page last reviewed: September 13, 2018. CDC.gov. https://www.cdc.gov/ncbddd/spinabifida/data.html (accessed December 12, 2018).
[84] Spina Bifida Family Support. "Abortion Of Disabled Babies Increasing at Alarming Rate." Published 2004. SPINABIFIDASUPPORT.com. http://www.spinabifidasupport.com/abortionrates.htm (accessed December 10, 2018).
[85] Ertelt, Steven. "Disability Discrimination: Killing Disabled Babies in Late-Term Abortions." Published 2013. LIFENEWS.com. http://www.lifenews.com/2013/11/25/disability-discrimination-killing-disabled-babies-in-late-term-abortions/ (accessed December 12, 2018).

advancements will continue to extend the life expectancy of those who suffer from the condition.

Abortion and Gender

Luckily for women, they, too, get to be the victims of abortion – and not just as expectant mothers! And as usual, liberals' favorite *cause célèbre* (abortion) hurts minorities (in this case baby girls from minority backgrounds) the most.

According to an article published in the magazine of the National Academy of Sciences (that organization was founded by congressional charter during the presidency of Abraham Lincoln, and publishes one of the most well-respected scientific journals in the world) "U.S.-born children of Chinese, Korean, and Asian Indian parents" are significantly more likely to be boys – especially if the parents have already had at least one girl.[86] Here's the breakdown:

1. In the case of a first child, there are generally 1.05 boys born for every girl.
2. In the case of a second, where the first child was a girl, there are 1.17 boys born for every girl.
3. Where the first two children were girls, 1.50 boys (nearly 50% more than the average number of boys in first births) are born to every girl.

As William Saletan correctly opined in his article on the study for *Slate* magazine: "There's no plausible innocent explanation for this enormous and directionally abnormal shift in probability. The authors conclude that the numbers are "evidence of sex selection, most likely at the prenatal stage.""[87]

---

[86] Saletan, William. "Fetal Subtraction Sex Selection in the United States." Published 2008. SLATE.com. http://www.slate.com/articles/health_and_science/human_nature/2008/04/fetal_subtraction.html (accessed December 12, 2018).

"At the prenatal stage." Or in other words, female babies are being aborted. Because the parents prefer boys. And here I thought liberals were against gender discrimination – I guess not, if it means less business for the abortion industry. Granted, no one ever thought they were *seriously* against murder in general, given the violent crime rates in almost every city Democrats control, but I'd have thought they would at least stand by their guns on gender inequality.[88]

And although we're mostly talking about abortion in the United States, it's worth noting that baby gender disparity is prevalent elsewhere in the world as well – at least where parents have the technology to use abortion (although occasionally parents simply kill female babies after they are born) to choose the gender of their child.

For example, in 2017 the *New York Times* reported that "There were 33.59 million more men than women in China in 2016, according to figures from the country's National Bureau of Statistics…".[89] This is in direct contrast to other developed nations such as the United States, whose census bureau reports only slightly higher percentages of women in the United States than men.[90]

---

[87] Saletan, William. "Fetal Subtraction Sex Selection in the United States." Published 2008. SLATE.com. http://www.slate.com/articles/health_and_science/human_nature/2008/04/fetal_subtraction.html (accessed December 12, 2018).

[88] Just kidding. They don't have any guns to stand by, literally or figuratively.

[89] Tatlow, Didi Kirsten. "In China, a Lonely Valentine's Day for Millions of Men." Published 2017. NYTIMES.com. https://www.nytimes.com/2017/02/14/world/asia/china-men-marriage-gender-gap.html (accessed December 12, 2018).

[90] United States Census Bureau. "We the People: Women and Men in the United States." Issued January 2005. CENSUS.gov. https://www.census.gov/prod/2005pubs/censr-20.pdf (accessed December 13, 2018).

As the *Times* also reported regarding China's gender disparity: "The reasons for the gap are well known: a traditional preference for boys, compounded by the "one child" policy instituted in 1979 that led millions of couples to abort female fetuses. Worried...the government changed the policy last year to permit all couples to have two children."[91]

It won't be enough, of course. Merely allowing a couple to have two children[92] doesn't really solve the problem of parents aborting a second child, if both that child and the first child were girls. Especially given traditional Chinese culture, which doesn't always even count female children in the total number of siblings someone has. In addition, just because the rules now allow most Chinese couples to have two children doesn't mean that all couples will, especially with some seeing that as an economic hardship.[93]

India faces a similar, if less dramatic, situation. In India, according to a 2011 census, there were 940 women to every 1,000 men.[94] That would mean that women would need to gain nearly 3.1 percentage points in total population numbers to even

---

[91] Tatlow, Didi Kirsten. "In China, a Lonely Valentine's Day for Millions of Men." Published 2017. NYTIMES.com. https://www.nytimes.com/2017/02/14/world/asia/china-men-marriage-gender-gap.html (accessed December 12, 2018).

[92] Phillips, Tom. "China ends one-child policy after 35 years." Published 2015. THEGUARDIAN.com. https://www.theguardian.com/world/2015/oct/29/china-abandons-one-child-policy (accessed December 12, 2018).

[93] Levin, Dan. "Many in China Can Now Have a Second Child, but Say No." Published 2014. NYTIMES.com. https://www.nytimes.com/2014/02/26/world/asia/many-couples-in-china-will-pass-on-a-new-chance-for-a-second-child.html (accessed December 13, 2018).

[94] Census 2011. "Sex Ratio in India." CENSUS2011.CO.in. http://www.census2011.co.in/sexratio.php (accessed December 13, 2018).

the balance, which is on par with what I have seen estimated elsewhere for India.[95]

And the reasons for the disparity are once again – gender discrimination, which India continues to struggle with (although improvements have been made). If Democrats wanted to fight real gender discrimination, they'd fight it in places like India and in the Muslim world (where it is far worse than it is in India, with women having few rights and facing a myriad of daily threats).

For example, in India, prior to gender-based abortions being legally banned, billboards used to advertise them. In 2017, Raka Ray, PhD, wrote: "When I was a young feminist doing my PhD, and I was working with feminist groups in Bombay, I actually saw signs that said "pay 5,000 rupees now rather than 50,000 rupees later," which meant, get the test, get an abortion if it's a female, because otherwise you'll have to pay 50,000 in dowry."[96] [97]

In 2017, CNN reported that, despite it being illegal in India for a doctor to even tell a woman the sex of her baby before it is born – precisely out of concern over abortion – the practice is commonplace, with potentially millions of such abortions every year.[98] [99]

---

[95] Asia Experts Forum. "Raka Ray on sex-selective abortions in India." Published 2017. ASIAEXPERTSFORUM.org. http://asiaexpertsforum.org/raka-ray-sex-selective-abortions-india/ (accessed December 14, 2018).
[96] *Ibid.*
[97] Katz, Neil Samson, Sherry, Marisa. "India: The Missing Girls A society out of balance." Published 2007. PBS.org. http://www.pbs.org/frontlineworld/rough/2007/04/the_missing_gir.html (accessed December 7, 2018).
[98] Wu, Huizhong. "Activists go undercover to expose India's illegal sex-selective abortions." Published 2017. CNN.com. https://www.cnn.com/2017/03/26/asia/india-feticide-sex-selective-abortion-girls/index.html (accessed December 7, 2018).
[99] Testimony of McElya, Jill, J.D. to the House Committee on Foreign

In 2011, Britain's primarily television and radio network, the BBC, reported on the story of a young woman in India whose life was made a living horror as a result of her not initially bearing a son. "Until her son was born, Kulwant's daily life consisted of beatings and abuse from her husband, mother-in-law, and brother-in-law. Once, she says, they even attempted to set her on fire."[100]

Of course, at least gender-selective abortions are banned in India. In the United States, they're not even illegal (except in eight states).[101]

Speaking of which, let's get back to the U.S.A.

Affairs. 2013. "India's Missing Girls." INVISIBLEGIRLPROJECT.org. http://invisiblegirlproject.org/wp-content/uploads/2016/04/Testimony.9.10.2013.pdf (accessed December 8, 2018).

[100] BBC News. "Where are India's millions of missing girls?" Published 2011. BBC.com. https://www.bbc.com/news/world-south-asia-13264301 (accessed December 7, 2018).

[101] Guttmacher Institute. "Abortion Bans in Cases of Sex or Race Selection or Genetic Anomaly." GUTTMACHER.org. https://www.guttmacher.org/state-policy/explore/abortion-bans-cases-sex-or-race-selection-or-genetic-anomaly (accessed December 7, 2018).

4.

Abortion and the Poor

Since many black and Hispanic communities in the United States struggle with poverty, it shouldn't come as a shock that abortion disproportionately affects the poor as well.

According to the Guttmacher Institute, 49% of abortion recipients had incomes below the federal poverty level[102] which as of 2017 was just $16,240 for a household of two people.[103]

Although 49% is technically a minority, bear in mind that it doesn't count, for example, a two-person household making $20,000 a year in which the woman had an abortion. I don't know about you, but I would still consider such a household to be poor. In Southern California, for example, it is very hard to find a decent apartment for less than $9,000 a year – nearly half of a $20,000 income. And don't forget the cost of the abortion itself, which one Planned Parenthood clinic advertises as ranging from $435-$995.[104] Needless to say, despite the hundreds of millions in federal funds they get, not to mention donations, Planned Parenthood is not a free clinic.

In fact, the Guttmacher Institute's website states that 75% of abortion patients in 2014 were poor or low income.[105]

---

[102] Guttmacher Institute. "Induced Abortion in the United States." Published 2018. GUTTMACHER.org. https://www.guttmacher.org/fact-sheet/induced-abortion-united-states (accessed December 7, 2018).
[103] Wissman, Lindsay. "2017 Federal Poverty Level Guidelines." Published 2017. PEOPLEKEEP.com. https://www.peoplekeep.com/blog/2017-federal-poverty-level-guidelines (accessed December 8, 2018).
[104] Planned Parenthood of Western Pennsylvania. "Fees for Services." PLANNEDPARENTHOOD.ORG. https://www.plannedparenthood.org/planned-parenthood-western-pennsylvania/patients/fees-services (accessed December 9, 2018).

Isn't it amazing how many groups of people there are (such as the poor) that Democratic Party leaders supposedly love, that they are fine with seeing decimated? And isn't it amazing how conservatives and Republicans, despite supposedly hating those very groups, are desperate to see more of their members brought into the world?

It's a miracle!

[105] Guttmacher Institute. "Induced Abortion in the United States." Published 2018. GUTTMACHER.org. https://www.guttmacher.org/fact-sheet/induced-abortion-united-states (accessed December 7, 2018).

5.

Lincoln vs. Clinton

Former president Bill Clinton once gave the American people a line on abortion that was just as morally bankrupt and insulting as anything said in defense of slavery, pre-civil war. He said that abortion should be safe, legal, and rare.[106] [107]

The thing is…if what is in the womb is not a person, who cares if abortion is rare? If what is in the womb even *might* be a person, how could any decent human want it to be legal?

That point is clearly expressed in the following quote (read it, and then I promise I'll explain why it's so important):

> "It is vital to assert that the question of personhood is the most important question in the debate over abortion, and that there is no other decision upon which the question of the legal, moral, or ethical right to abortion can rest. There can be no middle road on this issue. For the doctrine of someone's right to life is true, absolutely and eternally true, but it has no justification as attempted by *Roe*. Or perhaps I should say that whether it has such just application depends upon whether the unborn is a person or not a person. If he or she is not a

---

[106] Smith, Cameron. "'Safe, Legal and Rare;' Abortion is Detached from Reality." Published 2013. CHRISTIANPOST.com. https://www.christianpost.com/news/safe-legal-and-rare-abortion-is-detached-from-reality-94569/ (accessed December 10, 2018).
[107] Barringer, Felicity. "The 1992 Campaign: Campaign Issues; Clinton and Gore Shifted on Abortion." Published 1992. NYTIMES.com. https://www.nytimes.com/1992/07/20/us/the-1992-campaign-campaign-issues-clinton-and-gore-shifted-on-abortion.html (accessed December 10, 2018).

person, why in that case the one who is may, as a matter of individual liberty, do just as she pleases with her unborn child. But if the unborn child is a person, is it not a total destruction of their right not to be deprived of life to deny him or her the ability to live their life free from deadly interference?"[108]

Abraham Lincoln spoke those exact words – almost. Just substitute "slavery" for "abortion", etc. Either a slave is a person or not, he argued. There can be no middle road, because you can't have "half" of a person. If you have a person, you have to free them. If not a person, you cannot make any law protecting slaves, since they would be mere property.

The same is true for an unborn child. Either you have a child, or you don't.

But former president Bill Clinton didn't want to anger either liberals or social conservatives, so he lied, and suggested that Americans could have it both ways. They could (he said) work to make abortion rare, while still keeping it legal. They could legally sign off on the slaughter of millions every decade, while patting themselves on the back for being "morally opposed" to abortion.

They might even create a few government programs aimed at slightly reducing the number of abortions!

Either you are murdering a human being through abortion, or you are not. You can't have it both ways. Legalizing murder is evil – and it's even worse if you know enough to realize

---

[108] Abraham Lincoln (with me editing in the word "abortion" in place of "slavery" etc.) "Speech to the Illinois House of Representatives" in *The Civil War a Narrative Fort Sumter to Perryville* (New York: Vintage Books, 1958), pp. 26, 27.

that abortion isn't okay, and should be "rare" – as Bill Clinton claimed he did.

6

Playing God?

Liberals often accuse conservatives of "playing God" on the abortion issue, but that honor goes to liberals. They say that conservatives are "playing God" by claiming to know that the baby is fully human, and not just a cluster of cells.

Can you imagine the nerve of Republicans, to suggest that a pregnant woman is carrying a baby?

Laying aside the fact that liberals would let off a river of angry internet comments if we ever aborted a baby hippopotamus, the "playing God" line is just bad logic.

It's true that conservatives can't easily prove that a human being is bestowed with a soul at the moment of conception – thus becoming spiritually and morally more than a clump of cells. Science does at least make it clear that *life begins at the moment of conception*. Modern research and technology have allowed us to understand the process by which the baby receives a completely unique genetic code. Science has allowed us to observe the rapidly changing structure of a baby's earliest form. The cells involved are undeniably alive, certainly human and – if left undisturbed – will gift the world a newborn baby in nine months.

What conservatives are arguing is that, if no one knows the exact moment at which those tiny cells become a complete *person*, conservatives and Republicans want to stay on the side of *not murdering anyone*.

Democrats and liberals have no more proof than we do as to the exact moment at which a person becomes…a person. The difference is that, not knowing if what's in the womb at three months is a child, they err on the side of saying "go ahead and kill it."

Apparently, that's their definition of "Life, Liberty, and the Pursuit of Happiness."[109] They just forgot the "life" part.

[109] National Archives. "Declaration of Independence: A Transcription." Published: 1776. ARCHIVES.gov. https://www.archives.gov/founding-docs/declaration-transcript (accessed December 13, 2018).

7.

History on Their Side

Democrats also like to talk about how history will be on their side, as if future books on American politics had already been written.[110] [111] Maybe they think they will get to decide what those will say, much like the Clintons presumably get to decide what George Stephanopoulos says on the nightly news.

But what about actual history?

For one thing, I can't think of any set of circumstances where the mass slaughter of innocents – let alone children – is remembered as a good and desirable thing. So unless Democrats can think of any other type of mass murder they (and others) agree with, they'd better prepare to be "on the wrong side of history."

On the subject of abortion, a quick internet search or two will reveal Democrats trying to show that history has already sided with them on abortion, and that the modern pro-life movement is really just a historical aberration.

For example, they'll often quote one of America's Founding Fathers (Dr. Benjamin Rush) speaking about abortion in purely medical terms, without specifically condemning it. They then treat this tepid medical description as a full-throated

---

[110] Yagoda, Ben. "Is Obama Overusing the Phrase the Wrong Side of History? Are We All?" Published 2014. SLATE.com http://www.slate.com/blogs/lexicon_valley/2014/04/17/the_phrase_the_wrong_side_of_history_around_for_more_than_a_century_is_getting.html (accessed December 14, 2018).

[111] Graham, David. "The Wrong Side of 'the Right Side of History.'" Published 2015. THEATLANTIC.com. https://www.theatlantic.com/politics/archive/2015/12/obama-right-side-of-history/420462/ (accessed December 13, 2018).

endorsement – not just on behalf of Dr. Rush, but on behalf of the entire founding generation. This despite the fact that Dr. Rush never gave an opinion on the subject.

But in reality, the fight against abortion likely began almost as soon as somebody made the procedure popular or common.

Traditionally, for example, doctors have been required to take the Hippocratic Oath, originally written by the famous Greek physician (and founder of modern medicine) Hippocrates. The oath lays out the basic ethical groundwork for being a physician, and states:

> "I swear by Apollo the physician, and Asclepius, and Hygieia and Panacea and all the gods and goddesses as my witnesses, that, according to my ability and judgement, I will keep this Oath and this contract:
>
> To hold him who taught me this art equally dear to me as my parents, to be a partner in life with him, and to fulfill his needs when required; to look upon his offspring as equals to my own siblings, and to teach them this art, if they shall wish to learn it, without fee or contract; and that by the set rules, lectures, and every other mode of instruction, I will impart a knowledge of the art to my own sons, and those of my teachers, and to students bound by this contract and having sworn this Oath to the law of medicine, but to no others.
>
> I will use those dietary regimens which benefit my patients according to my greatest ability and judgement, and I will do no harm or injustice to them.

I will not give a lethal drug to anyone if I am asked, nor will I advise such a plan; and similarly, *__I will not give a woman a pessary to cause an abortion.__*

In purity and according to divine law will I carry out my life and my art.

I will not use the knife, even upon those suffering from stones, but I will leave this to those who are trained in this craft.

Into whatever homes I go, I will enter them for the benefit of the sick, avoiding any voluntary act of Impropriety or corruption, including the seduction of women or men, whether they are free men or slaves.

Whatever I see or hear in the lives of my patients, whether in connection with my professional practice or not, which ought not to be spoken of outside, I will keep secret, as considering all such things to be private.

So long as I maintain this Oath faithfully and without corruption, may it be granted to me to partake of life fully and the practice of my art, gaining the respect of all men for all time. However, should I transgress this Oath and violate it, may the opposite be my fate.[112]

As you can see, Hippocrates didn't like abortion, and forbade medical practitioners from participating in it. Clearly, he

---

[112] National Library of Medicine, National Institutes of Health, etc. "Greek Medicine." Translated 2002. NLM.NIH.gov. https://www.nlm.nih.gov/hmd/greek/greek_oath.html (accessed December 12, 2018). Emphasis added.

also disagreed with physician-assisted suicide – another favorite liberal way of eliminating those they consider "undesirable" or a "burden" on society.

And before Democrats continue their all-out support for abortion, and declare history "on their side" they might want to look at just who did support the practice historically.

The Nazis, for example, were abortion advocates.

Although some pro-abortion activists have tried to claim that the Nazis were against abortion, this was only true with regards to groups who fit into the Nazi worldview as being "desirable." In other words, the Nazis were happy to see people have lots of babies, if they liked the people in question, and the babies might one day grow up to serve in the German military.

For groups that the Nazis didn't like, they had no problem with abortion at all. According to the United States Holocaust Memorial Museum: "Pregnant Jewish women often tried to conceal their pregnancies or were forced to submit to abortions."[113] The museum also states that the same was true for other groups. For example:

> "Pregnancy sometimes resulted for Polish, Soviet, or Yugoslav forced laborers from sexual relations with German men. If so-called "race experts" determined that the child was not capable of "Germanization," the women were generally forced to have abortions, sent to give birth in makeshift nurseries where conditions would guarantee the death of the infants, or

---

[113] United States Holocaust Museum. "Women During the Holocaust." USHMM.org. https://www.ushmm.org/wlc/en/article.php?ModuleId=10005176 (accessed December 11, 2018).

simply shipped to the region they came from without food or medical care."[114]

The Nazis didn't like abortion. They loved it. It helped them eliminate groups they didn't like.

So, they and Democrats share that (a love for abortion) in common (in addition to being socialists – the Nazis were the National Socialist Worker's Party, after all.).

The murderous communists in Russia loved abortion, too, although it was banned for one twenty-year period (with the ban ending well before the *Roe* case ever made it legal in America). And it was legalized there for one of the same reasons liberals allegedly back it in America – gender "equality."

According to a 2017 article in *Foreign Policy*: "In 1920, in the spirit of gender equality, the Soviet Union became the first state in the world to legalize abortion, and the practice has remained popular ever since."[115]

For reference, the communist party (also known as the Bolsheviks) had started taking total control of Russia in 1917. What a shock that abortion almost immediately became the law of the land.

Granted, abortion was hardly the only mass slaughter that occurred under communism (which even Democrats admit represents the left side of the political spectrum). Under Joseph Stalin, former leader of the communist Soviet Union, even the lowest of estimates state that at least 10 million civilians were intentionally killed (not to mention countless deaths from bad

---

[114] *Ibid.*

[115] Ferris-Rotman, Amie. "Putin's Next Target Is Russia's Abortion Culture." Published 2017. FOREIGNPOLICY.com. http://foreignpolicy.com/2017/10/03/putins-next-target-is-russias-abortion-culture/ (accessed December 13, 2018).

leftist policies that may put the total dead at 40-60 million). Bear in mind that Stalin's reign represents only 39 percent of the Soviet Union's history, the rest of which was also filled with death and destruction across the globe.

And then there's King Herod from the Bible, another historical leader who was fine with murdering infants.

In his attempt to kill Christ, while Jesus was still a baby, Herod "ordered the massacre of all the boys in Bethlehem and its vicinity two years old and under..."[116]

It's interesting that the first gravely evil act we read about in the New Testament is the murder of babies. This particular act of Herod's now overshadows any other in terms of how he is remembered by history, even though he had a long and interesting reign.

Apparently, history often sides against baby killers. Who knew? Well, other than conservatives, Republicans, and those Christians who attend church weekly or more, and who vote Republican by overwhelming majorities.[117] [118]

---

[116] New American Bible. Matthew 2:16. Copyright 1987, 1981. 2002-2003 edition.

[117] CNN Election 2016. Exit Polls National President. Published 2016. CNN.com. https://www.cnn.com/election/2016/results/exit-polls (accessed December 14, 2018).

[118] In 2016, Trump defeated Clinton by 14 percentage points among voters who attended religious services weekly or more. He also defeated her by two points among those attended monthly, 49 to 47%. He lost by only two points among those who attended "a few times a year." He only lost by a substantial margin among those who "never" attended religious services – by thirty-two points. The lesson: take your kids and grandkids to church. It will affect their character.

8

How Abortion Affects Women – (Other Than Just Killing Them in the Womb). The Psychology and Physical Effect on Mothers

Not only was Bill Clinton spouting nonsensical garbage with his argument that abortion should be "legal and rare" but he was also wrong about saying it could be "safe."

Abortion has a host of negative side effects – many of which the medical community openly acknowledges. As with other things, the physical and psychological side effects on women have not stopped Democrats from supporting abortion, but by now that should come as no surprise.

What should come as a surprise is the failure of that same medical community to roundly condemn the practice of abortion, given some of the side-effects I'll go over below (not to mention the whole "killing of a human being" thing, and the violation of every doctor's "do no harm" creed). But whenever a member of the medical community steps forward to talk about the dangers involved, they are roundly ridiculed – including by people who aren't even doctors.

In dismissing concerns for the health of the mother, news organizations have said the following:

> Huffington Post – "[I]nduced abortion and miscarriage are the safest outcomes of pregnancy."[119] (Safest for whom is the question – certainly not the baby).

---

[119] Grimes, David A. "How Safe Is Abortion?" Published 2015, updated 2017. HUFFIGTONPOST.com https://www.huffingtonpost.com/david-a-grimes/how-safe-is-abortion_b_6391460 (accessed October 11, 2018).

CBS News – "Abortions in the U.S. are very safe but getting one without facing delays and false medical information depends on where women live..."[120]

NBC News – "Studies have also debunked the argument that abortions raise the risk of depression or breast cancer."[121]

NPR – "Abortions in the United States are safe and have few complications, according to a landmark new study..."[122]

Here some of real effects of abortion, to the extent that the medical community has bothered to study them (and to the extent to news organizations have bothered to report on them):

Psychological Effects of Abortion

Suicide

According to an article in *Psychology Today*,[123] in women who have had abortions, abortion often causes "Post Abortion Stress Syndrome." Some of the symptoms of this include:

---

[120] The Associated Press. "Abortions in U.S. are safe but some state laws pose risks, report says." Published 2018. CBSNEWS.com https://www.cbsnews.com/news/abortions-are-safe-but-some-state-laws-pose-risks-report-says/ (accessed October 2, 2018).
[121] Fox, Maggie. "Abortion in the U.S.: Five key facts." Published 2018. NBCNEWS.com. https://www.nbcnews.com/health/health-news/abortion-u-s-five-key-facts-n889111 (accessed October 11, 2018).
[122] Kodjak, Alison. "Landmark Report Concludes Abortion In U.S. Is Safe." Published 2018. NPR.org. https://www.npr.org/sections/health-shots/2018/03/16/593447727/landmark-report-concludes-abortion-is-safe (accessed October 11, 2018).
[123] Babbel, Susanne, Ph.D., M.F.T. "Post Abortion Stress Syndrome (PASS) - Does It Exist?" Published 2010. PSYCHOLOGYTODAY.com. https://www.psychologytoday.com/us/blog/somatic-psychology/201010/post-abortion-stress-syndrome-pass-does-it-exist (accessed October 10, 2018).

1. Guilt,
2. Anxiety,
3. Depression,
4. Flashbacks, and
5. Suicidal thoughts.

Suicidal thoughts. *Suicidal thoughts.* Sure, abortion is a great thing for women!

Apparently, killing female babies through abortion isn't the end of liberal sexism. As long as it serves their purpose, liberals are ok with it if adult women die – this time via suicide.

On a side note, liberal politicians don't even care about protecting fake women, as transgender individuals (supported in their "lifestyle" by liberals) have a 38-40% suicide rate,[124] [125] which remains roughly the same regardless of whether they receive the transgender surgeries they desire or not.

Other supposedly "victimized" minorities in American society do not have anything like a 40% suicide rate, with white Americans actually having among the highest rates.[126]

But why *would* liberals care if people die, as long as they can turn another group of potential voters (women, transgenders, etc.) towards "victim" mentality – which liberals

---

[124] Payne, Daniel. "The Transgender Suicide Rate Isn't Due To Discrimination." Published 2016. THEFEDERALIST.com. http://thefederalist.com/2016/07/07/evidence-the-transgender-suicide-rate-isnt-due-to-discrimination/ (accessed October 15, 2018).
[125] Ungar, Laura. "Transgender people face alarmingly high risk of suicide." Published 2015. USATODAY.com. https://www.usatoday.com/story/news/nation/2015/08/16/transgender-individuals-face-high-rates--suicide-attempts/31626633/ (accessed October 16, 2018).
[126] American Foundation for Suicide Prevention. "Suicide Statistics." AFSP.org. https://afsp.org/about-suicide/suicide-statistics/ (accessed October 18, 2018).

can then take advantage of? "Hey, we're your champions. Republicans will never accept you as you are, the bigots! The nerve of them, outlawing child murder or warning you about bad life choices! Just because this abortion/lifestyle might kill you, or lead to serious problems, doesn't mean you should have to endure listening to the truth!"

Mental Trauma Other Than Suicide

Even if the woman who just had an abortion *doesn't* commit suicide, what about some of the other problems listed in *Psychology Today*? Guilt, anxiety, depression, flashbacks. At what point is it better (not to mention more respectful of human life) to simply encourage women to bring life into the world, even if the circumstances aren't ideal?

Having a baby isn't the end of the world, even if it's not planned – and most parents will tell you they wouldn't trade their kids for anything.

And as hard as it is for a new mom, adoption is always an option.

Are children *that* bad for parents, that we have to have abortion available as a form of last-resort contraception? Are children really worse than the consequences of having an abortion?

Let's look at abortion's connection to depression.

A Danish study on women born in Denmark between the years 1980 and 1994 shows an 8% jump in the number of women who used anti-depressants before an abortion vs. after.[127]

---

[127] Rapaport, Lisa. "Abortion not tied to increased risk of depression." Published 2018. REUTERS.com. https://www.reuters.com/article/us-health-abortion-depression/abortion-not-tied-to-increased-risk-of-depression-idUSKCN1J134J (accessed October 21, 2018).

Now, if I told you that your child was 8% more likely to end up on anti-depressants if they watched more than 1 hour of TV a day, you'd take that seriously, right? If you believed me, you certain wouldn't say that "TV is not tied to increased risk of depression." You might even start sharply curtailing your child's TV time out of concern, because that would be the right thing to do.

The same is true regarding abortion and depression. If it's causing women to take anti-depressants, we should be concerned.

But guess what? A 2018 Reuters article (Reuters is one of the largest news organizations in the world) published the same Danish study under the following headline: "Abortion not tied to increased risk of depression."

What? Seriously? The article itself even stated:

> Women who had an abortion were 54 percent more likely to take antidepressants in the year after the procedure than women who didn't have abortions but were tracked for the same one-year period, the study found. But their increased use of antidepressants was already evident in the year before the abortions, when these women were 46 percent more likely to take antidepressants than their counterparts who didn't have abortions."[128]

So let's see... 54% minus 46% = 8%. An 8% increase in the number of women taking anti-depressants following abortion. The liberal media headline lied about the study, pure and simple.

But my favorite part is the fact that the article writers just brushed the whole thing aside (as seen above) by essentially

---

[128] *Ibid.*

saying "most of these women were on anti-depressants anyway, so who cares about the 8% increase?"

Shouldn't it at least concern them that 46% of women getting abortions were on anti-depressants to begin with? If almost half of all women who decide to abort their babies are depressed, shouldn't any doctor who has taken a basic psychology course (which is all of them) be concerned that the decision is one born of desperation, rather than informed and well-thought-out consent?

The article also tries to dismiss the 8% jump by saying it is not "statistically significant." Really? So, one more woman out of every twelve to thirteen needing to take anti-depressants isn't "statistically significant?"

In fact, according to the same article, only 15% of women overall are on anti-depressants, versus 54% of women who have had abortions.

Is that "statistically significant" enough for you, Reuters?

Sure, studies can have margins of error, but those often run around 3-4%, meaning 8% *is* statistically significant. Especially since, even if you assumed a margin of error of 8%, that would mean that the study could also have "randomly" shown women to be 8% *less* likely to be on anti-depressants after abortion. Instead, it showed they were 8% *more* likely. You can only verbally twist numbers just so far, before you're simply ignoring results

The point is, politicians on the left just don't care. They want abortion-on-demand, they want money from abortion doctors to fill their political campaign accounts, and they want women to feel like conservatives/Republicans are trying to take away their rights.

In pursuing that agenda, they don't care who gets hurt.

Project Rachel and Rachel's Vineyard

While some studies and media reports have claimed there is no link between abortion and depression (and the other symptoms *Psychology Today* mentioned), that simply doesn't fit the real-world facts.

In fact, many women seek direct help in dealing with the psychological after-effects of abortion.

Project Rachel is a Catholic group that helps both women and men recover emotionally after abortion. They currently operate on some level in almost every Catholic diocese (church district) in the United States. Thousands and thousands of women have been helped through their ministry, which has grown exponentially since its founding.

Through Rachel's Vineyard, a similar but unrelated[129] ministry, over 1,000 retreats with the same purpose are held *annually*, both inside and outside the U.S. These retreats help both men and women recover from the emotional aftermath of abortion.

Considering that Rachel's Vineyard held its first retreats in 1995, the expansion to over 1,000 per year (a mark hit within 19 years) is remarkable.

Nearly as remarkable is the fact that the retreats occur in no less than 70 different countries, including the U.S. Vicki Thorn, the founder of Project Rachel, noted to me in the course of a phone interview that:

1. The need for healing may be especially great in Eastern European countries that were formerly controlled by the Soviet Union (U.S.S.R.) such as Romania and Ukraine.

---

[129] Despite their similar names and missions, Rachel's Vineyard and Project Rachel are entirely separate groups.

2. In such countries, an extraordinarily high percentage of the female population may have had an abortion.

3. Some women there may have had dozens of abortion procedures (without even being certain if they are pregnant in any single case) as abortion in such countries is not-infrequently used as an almost casual birth-control method.[130]

Ah, the communist Soviet Union. Just another of liberalism's little gifts to the world. Liberalism seems to leave those kinds of gifts everywhere - the way pigeons leave gifts on the New York City sidewalk.

So, what are all these women (and men) doing attending retreats? Why are they seeking counseling? If you've never had an abortion, it would be pretty odd to attend a retreat that's supposed to help you recover from an abortion. Similarly, if you were frightened to have a baby, and then had an abortion with no substantial emotional consequences, one would think that the last thing you'd want to do with your weekend would be to spill your secrets to strangers, while receiving psychological help for something that didn't upset you.

Call me crazy, but that doesn't sound like fun. But who knows? Maybe liberals think these heartbroken men and women just want attention. Hollywood liberals can never get enough of it. Counseling services like those above are needed precisely because of the massive emotional harm abortion creates.

Even More Evidence of Psychological Harm

Although it's not always easy to find information on the effects abortion has on women, even liberal advocates of abortion essentially acknowledge that it can be psychologically harmful to women. For example:

---

[130] Vicki Thorn, phone interview with the author, August, 2018.

1. The Women's Clinic of Atlanta offers pre-abortion screening. An entire paragraph on their website is dedicated to "Possible Symptoms of Post Abortion Grief" which include, according to the clinic:
   - "Guilt, anxiety, or psychological numbness
   - Depression (unexplained feelings of sadness; sudden uncontrollable crying episodes; poor self-esteem; sleep or appetite disruption; reduced motivation; conflicts in relationships; thoughts of suicide)
   - Anniversary grief (on the anniversary date of the abortion or due date of the aborted child)
   - Flashbacks of the abortion
   - Preoccupation with becoming pregnant again or anxiety over fertility and childbearing issues
   - Interruption of the bonding process with other children
   - Survival guilt
   - Eating disorders, alcohol and drug abuse, or other self-punishing or self-degrading behaviors."[131]

Difficulty bonding with your other children? Eating disorders and drug abuse? Uncontrolled crying and thoughts of suicide? These are almost like the symptoms you would expect to see in a parent who lost a child. But I'm no doctor.

In truth, these symptoms are horrible. The Food and Drug Administration would never approve a medicine with these kinds of potential side-effects – yet abortion remains a celebrated medical procedure! Can you imagine if a potential drug had not only a high-potential for abuse, but could also cause:

1. Eating disorders,
2. Flashbacks,

---

[131] Women's Clinic of Atlanta. Post Abortion Care. WOMENSCLINICOFATLANTA.com. https://www.womensclinicofatlanta.com/post-abortion-care/ (accessed August 4, 2018).

3. Suicide,
4. Self-harm, and
5. Uncontrollable crying?

The lawyer side of me would love to be a part of THAT class-action lawsuit – when it was over, justice would be done, and I'd be filthy-stinking rich. In fact, I think a class-action lawsuit for failure to disclose the potential downsides of abortion could be the thing that shuts-down the abortion industry once-and-for-all. Hey, it did tremendous damage to Big Tobacco.

But wait, there's more!

An abortion provider in Miami requests on their website that you not bring children to their facility. Their illiterate site states "In consideration for our patients, emotional well being, please leave children home."[132]

Aside from the poor grammar (the statement should read "In consideration for our patients' emotional well-being, please leave children at home.") this statement says quite a lot. It says that they (the abortion provider) are afraid of losing business if a pregnant woman, upon seeing a child, decides that what is growing inside of her is, in fact, a human life.

And that's a significant admission. Abortion providers have told us over and over again that they simply want to give women a choice, and that they are careful to present women with options (including putting a child up for adoption).

Hiding something that could result in a woman thinking of her baby as human doesn't sound like the action of a

---

[132] Eve Women's Medical Centers. Pre-op and Post-op Patient Guidelines. EVEABORTIONCARESPECIALISTS.com. http://www.eveabortioncarespecialists.com/pre_care.html (accessed August 4, 2018).

concerned organization dedicated to providing "options." It sounds like a business trying to sell you on their product.

And then there's Planned Parenthood.

On the website for the Planned Parenthood of Western Pennsylvania, they are careful to state that "Neither the American Psychological Association nor the American Medical Association recognize post-abortion syndrome. For the majority of patients, emotional responses after an abortion are positive and women are able to move forward with their lives."[133]

And yet, this is in the context of their website's offer of Post Abortion Counseling. Just paragraphs later, the site states: "There are some women who do experience extreme negative reactions such as depression, shame, guilt or regret."[134]

But don't worry! The site lets you know that Planned Parenthood is there for you! If you're not completely satisfied with your emotional state, you have their money-back guarantee! Not! Actually, they offer counseling...for a mere $40 per session![135] That's right, for just a small fee, they can fix the hole they just created in your heart.

And here I was, thinking they didn't care.

Of course, because of how controversial abortion is (and because liberals are so defensive of it) it's hard to get funding to study abortion's negative effects. In the modern day, as we've already seen, even studies that show negative effects may be

---

[133] Planned Parenthood of Western Pennsylvania. Counseling Services. PLANNEDPARENTHOOD.org.
https://www.plannedparenthood.org/planned-parenthood-western-pennsylvania/patients/counseling-services (accessed August 4, 2018).
[134] *Ibid*.
[135] *Ibid*.

intentionally misreported. Others get "buried" (go unreported) or get very little attention.

But in the early going, sometimes the negative consequences of abortion did leak out.

One excellent example is a 1986 study by researchers working at the University of Minnesota. The researchers wanted to study the suicide rate in teenage girls who had undergone an abortion procedure.

The study concluded that teen girls who had had an abortion in the previous six months were six times more likely to commit suicide than their peers who had not.[136] Sixty suicides, then, among abortion recipients, for every ten among other young ladies. Six times the death count.

At that rate, what you have is not terribly well described as a correlation between abortion and suicide.

It's more like simple cause and effect.

Physical Problems after Abortion

As previously noted, major news cartels (eh, I mean, organizations!) love to tell the public how physically and emotionally safe abortion is. It obviously isn't safe for the baby, so I'll assume they're talking about the mother. But even when it comes to the *physical* safety for the mother, it's hard to find a non-dismissive conversation on the topic in the news, let alone a differing opinion.

---

[136] Reardon, David C., Ph.D. The Abortion/Suicide Connection. AFTERABORTION.org (Elliot Institute). http://afterabortion.org/1999/the-abortion-suicide-connection/ (Accessed August 4, 2018).

The thing is...why can't we talk about safety issues concerning abortion? As with so many things (global climate change, evolution, etc.) the Left is quick to insist that there can be only one opinion, and that anyone who disagrees is "anti-science."

As a conservative (or perhaps classical liberal) I dislike it when people on *either* side of the aisle simply dismiss issues and debates.

For example: I think the idea of man-made climate change has been highly exaggerated, and I know that China – not the US – is the main global polluter. But that doesn't mean I have zero concerns over what factories pump into the atmosphere, or am unwilling to listen to concerns about pollution.

By that same token, I don't understand why liberals won't even entertain the possibility that abortion should – medically speaking – be considered a risky procedure. Unless they have something to hide, or are getting a lot of money out of the abortion industry. Oh wait. They do. And they are.

So, let's hear from one of the few news organizations willing to cover the topic.

Quoting Dr. Donna Harrison, executive director of the American Association of Pro-Life Obstetricians and Gynecologists, the Catholic News Agency reported that "Abortion is not safe for women. Safe means free from risk, free from harm. And abortion harms women."[137]

Dr. Harrison specifically listed the potential physical side-effects as these:

---

[137] Maslak, Maggie. Is abortion really safe? "Critics respond to new study." Published 2018. CATHOLICNEWSAGENCY.com. https://www.catholicnewsagency.com/news/is-abortion-really-safe-critics-respond-to-new-study-34947 (accessed October 21, 2018).

1. Damage to the uterus,
2. Early birth in subsequent pregnancies (putting future children at risk),
3. Bleeding in pelvic organs and in the womb,
4. Breast cancer.[138]

Liberals often contest the breast-cancer claim, but Dr. Harrison explains specifically how the risk is created. Abortion, she says, "affects the maturity of breast tissue development, prematurely halting the production of milk and making the tissue more susceptible to cancer."[139]

In other words, rich Democrat politicians, who are utterly terrified that genetically-modified corn might enter their mouths for fear of getting cancer, have completely dismissed the possibility that interrupting a powerful natural process within the body could have negative side effects.

Maybe that's because they're not the ones getting the abortions.

Dr. Harrison's other claims make sense as well. If you use steel instruments to rip a baby apart during an abortion procedure (which abortionists routinely do) then of course there can be damage to the uterus. Of course there could be pelvic bleeding and inter-utero bleeding. And if you are forcing the womb to open prematurely, and potentially damaging it in the process, of course there is a risk of too-early births for subsequent children. Understanding these issues is not rocket science, it's common sense. On the other hand, dismissing their danger when you stand to profit from abortion is simply evil. And that takes us to our next topic: Abortion as an organized money racket.

---

[138] *Ibid.*
[139] *Ibid.*

9.

Abortion is a Racket – No Less than Organized Crime – Follow the Money

Contrary to what Democrats say, they – and abortion providers – want you to have as many abortions as possible. It's great business. Not just financially, but as noted, politically.

As I've pointed out previously, Planned Parenthood and other abortion clinics aren't offering free abortions. They're charging. $435-$995 per procedure, in fact.[140]

How does that work out in terms of profit for a doctor? Dr. Bernard Nathanson, a former abortion doctor who decided to become pro-life, said that during his career: "I had in fact presided over 60,000 deaths."[141] Even if the average cost of an abortion is just $500, that equals about $30,000,000 for any abortion doctor willing to work that much. That's $30 MILLION. And sure, the doctor has to pay his staff, and shell out for a few other expenses, but unless he's paying his nurse $300,000 per year (not a chance) the doctor is going to be *filthy rich*).

Think $30 million is a lot? I'm just getting started. Another former abortion doctor who eventually went pro-life claims he charged $250-500 per abortion.[142] Significantly less

---

[140] Planned Parenthood of Western Pennsylvania. Fees for Services. PLANNEDPARENTHOOD.org.
https://www.plannedparenthood.org/planned-parenthood-western-pennsylvania/patients/fees-services (accessed October 22, 2018).
[141] Grimes, William. "B. N. Nathanson, 84, Dies; Changed Sides on Abortion." Published 2011. NYTIMES.com.
https://www.nytimes.com/2011/02/22/us/22nathanson.html (accessed November 19, 2018).
[142] Terzo, Sarah. "Former abortionist describes how profitable abortion can be." Published 2015. LIVEACTION.org.
https://www.liveaction.org/news/former-abortionist-describes-

than Planned Parenthood now charges, right? Perhaps he was trying to help the poor?

Well, here's the thing. A first trimester abortion only takes about 5-15 minutes of the actual doctor's time[143] [144] (and as noted, late-term abortions cost more). So, assuming based on the numbers of the doctor above that there are places where you can get an abortion cheaper than at the "charitable" Planned Parenthood, let's assume the *average* abortion costs only $400. So that's:

A. $400, multiplied by
B. 6 ten-minute abortions in one hour, multiplied by
C. 8 work hours in a day, multiplied, by
D. 5 work days a week, multiplied by
E. 48 weeks per year (there are 52.14 weeks in a year, but we'll assume the "doctor" wants a month off every year!) multiplied by
F. 30 years of work (from, say, age 30-60) which equals
G. Lifetime earnings of $138,240,000.

That's 4.6 times more than my original $30 million estimate.

And that's assuming a month off every year, and retirement at age 60 (whereas many Americans do not retire until they are 65-70). And sure, doctors have to pay for medical insurance, and may not actually be able to fit that many abortions into the average day, but even if their lifetime profit is half of $138 million, they're still getting unbelievably rich.

---

profitable-abortion-can-doctors/ (accessed October 25, 2018).
[143] *Ibid.*
[144] Feminist Women's Health Center. "Frequently Asked Questions - About Abortion Appointments." FWHC.org.
https://www.fwhc.org/abortion/faq.htm (accessed October 25, 2018).

Of course, I can't be absolutely sure about the amount the average abortion doctor earns per year. For some reason, they don't seem to want to use my legal services for their taxes.

But even if we just go with thirty-million in lifetime earnings, think about the following.

What would you do for $30 million – an amount even many professional baseball players never accumulate in their careers? Probably more than you'd care to admit!

Due to baseball (MLB) rules, most players play the first 1-3 years of their careers making "only" around $0.55 million dollars per year. The average annual salary for players is around $4 million.[145] What that means: a professional ball player could easily have a 10-year career in the majors and still make less than $30 million, even assuming they got the MLB average every single year after their first three.

And unlike ballplayers, abortion practitioners get to work in an air-conditioned building, order their staff around, and talk about how they are performing a wonderful public service. No wonder they fight hard to defend their...profession.

What about Planned Parenthood's profit from abortion (you know, the organization that begs congress for of millions of your taxpayer dollars every year, and that performs more abortions than any other group or clinic)?

Well, Planned Parenthood claims to have done 327,653 abortions in just one recent year (Oct. 2012-Sep. 2013).[146] I'd bet

---

[145] The Associated Press. "Players' union: End-of-year average MLB salary a record $4M." Published 2017. USATODAY.com. https://www.usatoday.com/story/sports/mlb/2017/12/22/players-union-end-of-year-average-mlb-salary-a-record-4m/108856114/ (accessed October 23, 2018).
[146] Arter, Melanie. "Planned Parenthood: We Did 327,653 Abortions in One Year." Published 2015. CNSNEWS.com.

that's an underestimate, but we'll go with it. So let's see...that's at least $163,826,500.00. Per year. At a minimum. Not too shabby.

And then they *also* have the temerity to beg for public donations, *in addition to getting your tax money*, as if they were a charity! Can you imagine if any other $163.8 MILLION a year business asked for donations? They would be unmercifully mocked, and rightfully so!

Of course, Planned Parenthood would say they are not a business...which mostly means that they don't even have to pay taxes on their ill-gotten gains (they are classified as a "nonprofit" organization). But does being in a "nonprofit" mean that you can't make a *boatload* of money? Oh, you can make *lots* of money working for a nonprofit – In fact, high-level executives at Planned Parenthood do quite nicely each year.

For example, according to the well-respected Washington Examiner, Cecile Richards, the former boss of Planned Parenthood, made a salary of $957,952.[147] I suspect that the only reason it wasn't a million was so that it wouldn't sound quite as bad if anyone inquired.

Does anyone really believe that none of the abortion money swirling around finds its way back to the Democratic Party, their candidates, or their causes? Or believe that such campaign help isn't a huge reason why Democrats fiercely defend the industry and vice-versa? Without Democrats, the abortion industry would be sunk, so I'm going to guess the money does

https://www.cnsnews.com/news/article/melanie-hunter/planned-parenthood-we-did-327653-abortions-one-year (accessed October 30, 2018).
[147] Bedard, Paul. "Report: Planned Parenthood HQ average exec salary $389,514." Published 2017. WASHINGTONEXAMINER.com. https://www.washingtonexaminer.com/report-planned-parenthood-hq-average-exec-salary-389-514 (accessed October 10, 2018).

find its way to Democratic campaign coffers. Actually, I don't have to guess.

You see, according to USA Today: "In fact, since 2012, Planned Parenthood alone has donated virtually the same amount ($2.6 million) to individual candidates as the NRA [National Rifle Association] ($2.7 million) has."[148]

And that's just to individual candidates. That doesn't include any donations to left-leaning organizations, or the fact that Planned Parenthood routinely publishes left-leaning stories and information clearly designed to influence voters.

For example, the Twitter feed of Planned Parenthood's tax exempt 501(c)(4) organization (which under the tax code means an organization dedicated strictly to "social welfare") put out the following political tweets in just the three hours prior to my writing this:

1. Attempting to influence the governor of Ohio: "Two dangerous & unconstitutional abortion bans are making their way through the Ohio Statehouse today. We anticipate both will be on their way to Gov. @JohnKasich's desk this week. TAKE ACTION to #StopTheBans."

2. Against a Trump judicial nominee: "If Jonathan Kobes is confirmed, it would mean weaker rights and less access to health care for women across the nation, warns Sen. @PattyMurray. The Senate will begin voting on his nomination in 30 minutes. Kobes

---

[148] Schneider, Christian. "If the NRA owns Republicans, Planned Parenthood owns Democrats." Published 2018. USATODAY.com https://www.usatoday.com/story/opinion/2018/02/26/if-nra-owns-republicans-planned-parenthood-owns-democrats-christian-schneider-column/372679002/ (accessed October 25, 2018).

doesn't belong on the federal bench. #courtsmatter #StopKobes."

3. Praising a Democratic Party Senator: "@SenatorHeitkamp, our deepest gratitude for always fighting to protect our health care and for believing survivors. You've shown what it takes to vote your values. Thank you."[149]

At least the NRA, which donates most of its campaign money to Republicans, doesn't kill anyone (whatever you may think of gun rights, no one is employed by the NRA to walk around killing babies, or anyone else for that matter).

According to the same article in the Washington Examiner referenced above, *thirty-three* other CEOs at Planned Parenthood made at least a sweet $200,000 per year.[150]

For some context, according to the government's Census Bureau, the median American household income in 2017 was $61,372.[151] That's *household* income. So, assuming there are at least two working adults in any given house (a mother/father, mother/son, grandmother/granddaughter, whatever) the average person in that house is making just over $30,000 per year.

All while Cecile Richards makes nearly a cool $1 million working for a "nonprofit." Her husband also works (although not

---

[149] Planned Parenthood Action. Twitter Account. TWITTER.COM. https://twitter.com/PPact (accessed December 11, 2018).

[150] Bedard, Paul. "Report: Planned Parenthood HQ average exec salary $389,514." Published 2017. WASHINGTONEXAMINER.com. https://www.washingtonexaminer.com/report-planned-parenthood-hq-average-exec-salary-389-514 (accessed October 10, 2018).

[151] Fontenot, Kayla, Semega, Jessica, Kollar, Melissa. "Income and Poverty in the United States: 2017." Published 2018. CENSUS.gov. https://www.census.gov/library/publications/2018/demo/p60-263.html (accessed October 25, 2018).

at Planned Parenthood) so it's not as if the family has to survive solely on Cecile's income.

Oh, and if you still don't believe that the Richards family and the abortion industry are in bed with the Democratic Party, Cecile Richards' daughter, Lily, was the press secretary for Tim Kaine – Hillary Clinton's 2016 running mate, and the former governor of Virginia. And Cecile's mother, also a Democrat, is the former governor of Texas.

Sex Trafficking and Abortion

But it gets so much worse. Abortion Providers aren't just money grubbing and sleazy – there's evidence that they are actually in bed with organized crime – including the sex trafficking of young girls.[152] [153]

According to a May 2018 report by the pro-life group Live Action, "Planned Parenthood is neglecting to report instances of sexual abuse to the authorities and in some cases sent their victims back to their abusers after performing an abortion."[154]

Now to be clear, Planned Parenthood is a mandated reporter. What that means legally is that, if they have *any*

---

[152] Wise, Talia. "'Back in the Arms of Her Predator': Why Traffickers and Abusers Send Young Girls to Planned Parenthood." Published 2018. 1.CBN.com. http://www1.cbn.com/cbnnews/us/2018/june/back-in-the-arms-of-her-predator-why-traffickers-and-abusers-send-young-girls-to-planned-parenthood (accessed December 22, 2018).
[153] Live Action. "Aiding Abusers." Published 2018. LIVEACTION.org. https://www.liveaction.org/wp-content/uploads/2018/05/Planned%20Parenthood%20Sexual%20Abuse%20Report%202018.pdf (accessed December 1, 2018).
[154] Wise, Talia. "'Back in the Arms of Her Predator': Why Traffickers and Abusers Send Young Girls to Planned Parenthood." Published 2018. 1.CBN.com. http://www1.cbn.com/cbnnews/us/2018/june/back-in-the-arms-of-her-predator-why-traffickers-and-abusers-send-young-girls-to-planned-parenthood (accessed December 22, 2018).

reasonable cause to suspect abuse of a child, *they must report it to law enforcement.*

Here were some examples regarding Planned Parenthood's failures (according to the report):[155]

1. In California in 2010, Edgar Ramirez got his 13-year-old daughter pregnant – twice – after raping her over the course of over seven months. In each case, she went to Planned Parenthood to get an abortion. In at least the second case, Edgar went with her. Despite the fact that 13-year-olds cannot legally consent to sex, there was no indication that Planned Parenthood ever reported the abuse.

2. In a 2014 report on sex trafficking by Loyola University Chicago,[156] Planned Parenthood was listed as the most-visited treatment facility for victims. When asked why she was taken by her abusers to Planned Parenthood one sex trafficking victim responded: "Because they didn't ask any questions."
Needless to say, this is significant evidence of Planned Parenthood's possible unspoken alliance with organized crime, as Planned Parenthood gets hundreds of dollars for every abortion they perform, thus benefiting

---

[155] Live Action. "Aiding Abusers." Published 2018. LIVEACTION.org. https://www.liveaction.org/wp-content/uploads/2018/05/Planned%20Parenthood%20Sexual%20Abuse%20Report%202018.pdf (accessed December 1, 2018). *Note* As I do not have personal knowledge of the incidents in Live Action's report, I am simply listing things from the report, to give people the opportunity to examine the report's validity, and make up their own minds.
[156] Loyola is ranked well within the top 1/3 of American National Universities by U.S. News and World Report, despite many universities not even being listed. U.S. News and World Report. Best Colleges, Loyola University Chicago. USNEWS.com. https://www.usnews.com/best-colleges/loyola-university-chicago-1710 (accessed October 26, 2018).

enormously from the business of any sex traffickers who walk through their doors.

3. In more than one case, Planned Parenthood staff counseled/told investigators posing as girls as young as 13-14 to lie about the circumstances of their pregnancy (supposedly the result of sex with older men) in order to get around parental notification laws, and potentially other laws as well.

4. Investigators posing *as sex traffickers* were told how to get abortions and STD tests *for their underage victims.* Planned Parenthood claimed, after this evidence (including a video!) was released that they had reported these Incidents. However, after filing a Freedom of Information Act Request, Live Action reported that, out of the five states and Washington, DC, where their undercover investigations had occurred, only one state showed any reports of a suspected crime. Again, this is suggestive of a link between the abortion giant and organized crime.

And on and on the report goes. Case after case. If you want to read it for yourself, the link to the page that connects to it is in my footnotes, and I'll add it here as well:

- https://www.liveaction.org/wp-content/uploads/2018/05/Planned%20Parenthood%20Sexual%20Abuse%20Report%202018.pdf

Quite frankly, it's not even clear where to go from there. Possible links to sex traffickers? Complete and total disregard for the sexual safety of young girls? This kind of thing is about as bad as it gets. But if you want to see Democrats lose their minds, try taking funding for this organization out of Congress' latest bloated spending bill. They'll defend their golden cash-providing calf as if it were their god.

Which of course, it is.[157]

In fact, just proceed to this next chapter to read the comments/acts of some prominent Democrats regarding attempts to defund Planned Parenthood (despite the fact that the concerns about the organization detailed in the above report actually did make front-page headlines – score one for the mainstream media!!!). You'll see for yourself just how much of a sacred cow this has become for them...

Democrats on De-funding Planned Parenthood

1. Hillary Clinton: "It shows not only an indifference, an insensitivity, maybe an obliviousness to what Planned Parenthood does for millions of women, but it also sends a message to the world that we can't govern ourselves..."[158]
2. Barack Obama: "The Obama administration has issued a final rule aimed at preventing state lawmakers from cutting funding for Planned Parenthood or other clinics that provide abortions."[159] – U.S. News and World Report
3. House of Representatives Democratic Leader Nancy Pelosi: "[T]o minister to the needs of God's creation is an act of worship. To ignore those needs is to dishonor the God who made us..."[160] So again, apparently de-funding Planned-Parenthood is dishonoring God?

---

[157] "You shall have no other gods before me." It's the very first commandment, but Democrats will break it in favor of Planned Parenthood any day of the week.

[158] Fraser-Chanpong, Hannah. "Clinton blasts Republican "partisanship" on Planned Parenthood." Published 2015. CBSNEWS.com. https://www.cbsnews.com/news/clinton-blasts-republican-partisanship-planned-parenthood/ (accessed October 30, 2018).

[159] Leonard, Kimberly. "Obama Administration Moves to Protect Planned Parenthood Funding." Published 2016. USNEWS.com. https://www.usnews.com/news/articles/2016-12-14/obama-administration-blocks-states-from-defunding-planned-parenthood (accessed October 30, 2018).

[160] Carr, Grace. "Nancy Pelosi Says Republicans 'Dishonor God' by Defunding Planned Parenthood." Published 2017. DAILYCALLER.com.

4. Democratic Senate Leader Chuck Schumer: "Trumpcare cuts @PPFA [Planned Parenthood] funds, hurting millions of women for mammograms, maternity care, cancer screenings & more."[161] [162] This by the way, is a lie – even the leftist Washington Post declared, specifically in reference to Schumer's words, that Planned Parenthood does not provide mammograms, and that at best only 7% of its activities are related to cancer screening.[163]

5. Senator Bernie Sanders: "The current attempt to discredit [and defund] Planned Parenthood is part of a long-term smear campaign by people who want to deny women in this country the right to control their own bodies..."[164]

6. Senator Cory Booker: He also strongly opposed defunding the abortion giant. You can watch his remarks

---

https://dailycaller.com/2017/06/30/nancy-pelosi-says-republicans-dishonor-god-by-defunding-planned-parenthood/ (accessed October 31, 2018).

[161] Chuck Schumer. Twitter Account. TWITTER.com. https://twitter.com/SenSchumer/status/839210602342019072?ref_src=twsrc%5Etfw%7Ctwcamp%5Etweetembed%7Ctwterm%5E8392106023 42019072&ref_url=https%3A%2F%2Fwww.washingtonpost.com%2Fne ws%2Ffact-checker%2Fwp%2F2017%2F03%2F09%2Fschumers-claim-that-millions-of-women-turn-to-planned-parenthood-for-mammograms%2F (accessed October 30, 2018).

[162] Ye Hee Lee, Michelle. "Schumer's claim that 'millions of women turn' to Planned Parenthood for mammograms." Published 2017. WASHINGTONPOST.com. https://www.washingtonpost.com/news/fact-checker/wp/2017/03/09/schumers-claim-that-millions-of-women-turn-to-planned-parenthood-for-mammograms/?utm_term=.dd9112da94f8 (accessed October 31, 2018).

[163] *Ibid*.

[164] Lavender, Paige. "Bernie Sanders: GOP Efforts To Defund Planned Parenthood 'An Attack On Women's Health'." Published 2015. HUFFINGTONPOST.com. https://www.huffingtonpost.com/entry/bernie-sanders-planned-parenthood_us_55b8f386e4b0074ba5a6fe60 (accessed October 31, 2018).

here
https://www.youtube.com/watch?v=slMKvgmVmhk, but
as they're rather long-winded and scatter-brained, I'm
not going to type them out.

7. Joe Biden, former vice-president: "And now these guys
   pledge that they are going to defund Planned
   Parenthood, which under law cannot perform any
   abortion..."[165]

Every high-ranking Democrat will defend Planned
Parenthood's funding to the death. Without its cash and
outspoken support, they might start losing elections!

Next, let's address the elephant in Joe Biden's room –
regarding the last quote on this list. Obviously, as America's
largest abortion provider, Planned Parenthood can perform
abortions.

What Biden may have meant was that they technically
can't use federal funds to perform abortions. This is and oft-used
argument by liberals, and it's also nonsense.

Let's say that your parents give you $100,000, but tell you
can't use it to buy a house. So instead you use it to pay for your
car, groceries, health insurance, and family vacations for the next
couple of years. This allows you to save enough money to buy a
house. So basically...the money went toward a house.

That's what happens when the government gives money
to Planned Parenthood, but says they can't use it for abortions.
Do they put the toward other things? Maybe! But with the

[165] Jeffrey, Terence P. "Biden: Planned Parenthood 'Under Law Cannot
Perform Any Abortion;' Planned Parenthood: We Did 985,731 In 3
Years." Published 2012. CNSNEWS.com.
https://www.cnsnews.com/news/article/biden-planned-parenthood-
under-law-cannot-perform-any-abortion-planned-parenthood-we
(accessed October 31, 2018).

money saved on those other things, they can then perform more abortions, open more abortion facilities, buy more abortion equipment, and pay staff at abortion facilities. It's not possible to give money to someone and then try to dictate what they spend it on. Even if they genuinely use it only as you intended, the money saved on those projects will inevitably go toward things you didn't want.

10.

The Gruesomeness of the Procedure

I'm sorry, I'm not going to do it. There have been plenty of books written on how the baby can actually feel pain, how the child will try to move away from the cold instruments about to rip them apart, and about what babies look and act like at various stages of development. The truth is, I don't have the heart for it.

So I'm a bit of a softie. Sue me. Actually, don't. I'm a lawyer, and I wouldn't want the other lawyers to find out I have feelings. I *do* have a reputation to uphold.

If you really want to know, the internet has a lot of information on the topic. One good and easy-to-use resource can be found at https://www.lifesitenews.com/resources/abortion, which offers simple information on baby development, abortion methods, and more.

Other sites that can easily searched show the horrifying pictures of fully-formed, murdered babies, and detail other aspects of the terrible procedures involved.

Let's move on.

11.

From a Biblical Perspective

There is significant debate even among Christians as to whether abortion is Biblically acceptable. Many of the faithful doubt that the Bible gives us any clear idea of when life begins. And it's true that the Bible doesn't specifically say (for example) "Life begins at conception!"

But that shouldn't surprise us, or cause us to doubt the divinely precious nature of human life, even in its earliest stages. In fact, it's safe to say that the Bible is clear on this topic. Here's why:

For one thing, it would have been very odd if Biblical authors had written about the moment of conception, since that moment in a pregnancy was a complete mystery at the time. Only modern microscopes, often combined with other advanced equipment, have allowed us to see egg and sperm cells. What's more, even eight weeks into a pregnancy, human children only have the weight of a large paper-clip, and measure just longer than half an inch. Thus, the entire first month or two of pregnancy has been a complete mystery for almost all of human history.

Second, abortion, while known in Biblical times, was not causing millions of global deaths per year, as it does today. In the ancient world, having a lot of healthy children to help with the family business or farm was normally seen as a huge blessing, so there was significantly less demand for *any* form of birth control. And as a result of abortion being fairly uncommon, it was not a primary topic of discussion among Jewish or early Christian theologians.

But all of that still begs the question, what *does* the Bible have to say about the early stages of life? Several things, it turns out.

Let's start with John the Baptist, whose preaching helped pave the way for Christ's ministry, and who personally baptized Jesus.

Early in the Gospel of Luke we learn that Mary, who was pregnant with Jesus at the time, visited Elizabeth her relative,[166] who was pregnant with John. Mary enters Elizabeth's house, and then something incredible happens.

> "When Elizabeth heard Mary's greeting, the infant leaped in her womb, and Elizabeth, filled with the Holy Spirit, cried out in a loud voice and said, "Most blessed are you among women, and blessed is the fruit of your womb. And how does this happen to me, that the mother of my Lord should come to me? For at the moment the sound of your greeting reached my ears, the infant in my womb leaped for joy.""[167]

What can we take away from this passage?

First, let's talk about the meaning and significance of John leaping for joy. Mathematically, we know that Elizabeth was in either the first or second trimester of her pregnancy when the baby in her womb leaped for joy – both periods in the pregnancy during which abortion is common, as discussed above. How do we know she was so early in her pregnancy? Well, we are told that "Mary remained with [Elizabeth] about three months..."[168]

---

[166] New American Bible. Luke 1:36. Copyright 1987, 1981. 2002-2003 edition.
[167] New American Bible. Luke 1:41-44. Copyright 1987, 1981. 2002-2003 edition.
[168] New American Bible. Luke 1:56. Copyright 1987, 1981. 2002-2003

Not only is there no indication that John was born during those three months, but the Gospel of Luke discusses the birth of John immediately *after* explicitly stating that Mary had gone home. So, assuming a roughly nine-month pregnancy, Elizabeth could not have been more than six months pregnant when Mary showed up.

In other words, the Bible explicitly states that at least three months before a normal pregnancy is finished, a baby is capable of feeling joy. That's a pretty good indication that God created unborn babies as fully-fledged human beings, even early in the pregnancy. That's especially true considering that, unless Elizabeth gave birth the day after Mary left, her unborn child would have been even younger than six months.

A second takeaway from the above passage (and scripture in general) is this: The Bible appears to support the idea that a child just-conceived is a fully-fledged human being, and as vital to God's plan for the universe as you or I.

Of course, the mere fact that Jesus was conceived and born as a human baby should strongly discourage any Christian from supporting or wanting to legalize abortion, but the above passage helps show that the soul of Jesus (and thus presumably the soul of any human child) was fully present in the womb from the very start. If this were not the case, why would John have *leaped for joy*? Why would Elizabeth have said "[B]lessed is the fruit of your womb."? Because Mary had a bunch of meaningless cells gathered in a clump in her abdomen? I don't think so. Such signs from the Holy Spirit filling Elizabeth could only have come as a reaction to the genuine presence of Jesus within Mary. And if Jesus was present in Mary from the beginning of her pregnancy, that creates a strong biblical case for life from the moment of conception.

edition.

But how do we know that Mary wasn't fairly late in her pregnancy by this point? What evidence is there that she was at the beginning of her pregnancy?

Well, as with John, we can't be sure of the exact date on which the baby was conceived, but we have quite a few clues. For one thing, in the Gospel of Luke, the Angel of the Lord announces to Mary that she will have a child in the passages immediately before Mary is described as visiting Elizabeth. That alone is significant evidence that she was at the beginning of her pregnancy when she visited her relative. In fact, the very next section after the angel's announcement to Mary tells us that Mary visited Elizabeth "during those days", i.e., during the days after the angel came to her. This is even *stronger* evidence that Mary wasn't very far along when she visited Elizabeth.[169]

We also know that the birth of Jesus is discussed in the Bible *after* the birth of John, whose mother was at most six months into her pregnancy when Mary visited her (see above). So, we know for sure that Mary was a maximum of six months into her pregnancy when she greeted Elizabeth, because she does not appear to have given birth until after Elizabeth did. And unless Mary gave birth the *day* after Elizabeth did, and unless Elizabeth was as far along as she possibly could have been when Mary visited her, it is highly likely that Mary was – at most – around halfway through her pregnancy when the presence of Jesus in her womb caused the reactions in Elizabeth and John.

And I think we can definitively show that Mary was even earlier in her pregnancy than the halfway point. Remember, she could not have had her baby immediately after departing from Elizabeth. This is because she would first presumably have had to go home and then travel (as Luke chapter two specifies) from Nazareth to Bethlehem. Bethlehem would, depending on the

---

[169] New American Bible. Luke 1:26-39. Copyright 1987, 1981. 2002-2003 edition.

roads and their condition, have been around an eighty to ninety-mile trip from Nazareth. Even the best transportation available at that time (such as a horse) could not have made such a journey in under several days – especially not if burdened with a rider and loaded with supplies. And there is no Biblical evidence that Mary and Joseph even had a donkey (as they are often portrayed as having in movies).

In short, there is powerful evidence in the above passage, and in the Gospel of Luke in general, that the soul of Jesus was fully present in Mary from the beginning of her pregnancy. For Christians, that should be a strong reason to take a pro-life stand.

What other evidence does the Bible contain that life in the womb is to be respected?

One of my favorite pro-life passages is Jeremiah 1:5 – "Before I formed you in the womb I knew you, before you were born I dedicated you, a prophet to the nations I appointed you."[170] What meaning should we draw from this passage?

The very first meaning I would have someone draw from this passage is that God loves them. He has a place and an important purpose for each of us *even before we are formed in the womb.*

But if God has a special place for each person even before they are conceived, how is it that any Christian dares to destroy an innocent person *after* they are conceived? How is it that any Christian would wish such a destruction of human life – no less a life than that of an adult person – to remain legal? That calls for serious thought, especially for Christians who routinely vote for pro-abortion politicians. And for those Christians who base their views of the subject on individual liberty, I would note that

---

[170] New American Bible. Jeremiah 1:5. Copyright 1987, 1981. 2002-2003 edition.

murder is neither a human nor a constitutional right, whether it presents itself as abortion or as the homicide of a clerk during a bank robbery.

Finally, there are these passages to consider:

- "But when [God], who from my mother's womb had set me apart and called me through his grace, was pleased to reveal his Son to me, so that I might proclaim him to the Gentiles, I did not immediately consult flesh and blood...." – Galatians 1:15-16.[171] Here we see Paul saying that he had been created to preach the Word of God to the Gentiles before he was even born. Paul is the Bible's great missionary – the one who really takes the Gospel outside of the Jewish community to the rest of the world. If he had never been born – if he had been lost in the womb – we have no guarantee that Christianity would have spread much beyond the Jewish community at all.
- "Be fertile and multiply..." – Genesis 1:28[172]
- "Children too are a gift from the Lord..." – Psalm 127:3[173]
- "You formed my inmost being; you knit me in my mother's womb. I praise you, so wonderfully you made me; wonderful are your works! My very self you knew; my bones were not hidden from you, When I was being made in secret, fashioned as in the depths of the earth. Your eyes foresaw my actions; in your book all are written down; my

---

[171] New American Bible. Copyright 1987, 1981. 2002-2003 edition.
[172] *Ibid.*
[173] *Ibid.*

days were shaped, before one came to be."
Psalm 139:13-16[174]

Abortion – from a Christian perspective – is simply wrong.

But there's one more point that's worth making in this section – and I address this to Catholics.

The Catholic Church is the largest single denomination in the United States – and about half of Catholics, according to exit polls, routinely support and vote for Democrats. And that's not acceptable.

The Catechism of the Catholic Church – effectively the Church's rule-book for believers – has this to say on the subject of abortion: "Human life must be respected and protected absolutely from the moment of conception. From the first moment of his existence, a human being must be recognized as having the rights of a person – among which is the inviolable right of every innocent being to life."[175]

The Catechism goes on to say the following regarding abortion: "When a state [government] does not place its power at the service of the rights of each citizen...the very foundations of a state based on law are undermined...the law must provide appropriate penal [criminal] sanctions for every deliberate violation of the child's rights."[176]

Translation: The church believes that laws should be passed subjecting doctors who continue to perform abortions in defiance of those laws to criminal punishment, and that if a government refuses to outlaw abortion its [the government's]

---

[174] *Ibid.*
[175] Catechism of the Catholic Church. Life in Christ/Abortion. Abortion (United States, New York: Image, 1994, 1997), p. 606, section 2270.
[176] Catechism of the Catholic Church. Life in Christ/Abortion. Abortion (United States, New York: Image, 1994, 1997), p. 607, section 2273.

very foundations are undermined. In short, it might not be a valid government, and its citizens may be entitled to practice civil disobedience in refusing to obey the government's laws on abortion.

Catholics need to stop voting for pro-abortion politicians. When? Yesterday.

12

Conclusion

I know it seems like I've been hard on liberals and Democrats in this book. I have. The reason is because I want them to repent of the evil that they've been doing or supporting (and yes, because occasionally we should have a good laugh over the absurdity of their ideas – if you don't learn to laugh, you'll only ever cry, especially over a topic like this one).

The truth is that the Gospel of Jesus Christ – in which I deeply believe – is a message of mercy. We are all sinners, all in need of God's mercy. I believe that the majority of Christian conversions happen through one-on-one conversations (although unlike everything else I've said in this book, I'm not giving a data-filled footnote to back that up). And so, I believe that our main goal is to always bring the person right in front us closer to God, and to the truth.

The purpose of this (sometimes snarky) work is not to condemn those who support abortion, have had abortions, or even those who perform abortions. It is to expose a grave error in the hope that they themselves will be forced to deal with the evil that plagues their lives, and our nation.

On the off chance that those performing abortions don't read this book, the other purpose is to arm you, the reader, with the arguments and knowledge you need to take down our nation's greatest sin. *A la lucha.* To the fight.

Oh, and one final suggestion. If you want to help the cause of life, it's a good idea to carry information – in your phone, wallet, or purse – on where a woman can get help during an emergency pregnancy (just make sure the place or resource in question operates from a religious and pro-life perspective, so that it will not simply direct a woman in crisis to an abortion doctor).

14.

Additional Resources

Here are some additional resources and information – specifically updates, websites, videos, and stories – for the reader to pursue if they want to learn more.

Legal Updates

As this was being written, several states have passed or attempted to pass truly horrific pro-abortion legislation. New York now allows non-doctors to perform abortions, and allows abortions to be performed up to the moment of birth in certain cases. It also allows abortions to go forward even when not medically necessary up to nearly six months into the pregnancy.[177] Virginia has also tried to pass legislation that could allow babies to be aborted up to the moment of birth[178] and Illinois is now about to pass legislation that would do just that.[179]

Awesome pro-life videos to share

While this book makes some good pro-life arguments (if I don't say so myself) video can be pretty moving, and a great way

---

[177] Desanctis, Alexandra. "The Indefensible Morality of Andrew Cuomo." Published 2019. NATIONALREVIEW.COM. https://www.nationalreview.com/2019/01/andrew-cuomo-new-york-abortion-law/ (accessed March 6, 2019).

[178] Pappas, Alex, "Outrage as video shows Virginia abortion bill sponsor saying plan would allow termination up until birth." Published 2019. FOXNEWS.com. https://www.foxnews.com/politics/outrage-after-virginia-abortion-bill-sponsor-admits-pregnancies-could-be-terminated-up-until-birth (accessed March 6, 2019).

[179] Parke, Caleb. "Illinois bill will make state the 'abortion capital of America,' pro-life group warns." Published 2019. FOX32CHICAGO.com. http://www.fox32chicago.com/news/national/illinois-bill-will-make-state-the-abortion-capital-of-america-pro-life-group-warns (accessed March 6, 2019).

to motivate others. It can also produce some laughs. So, for your entertainment and education (and that of your friends) here are some great pro-life videos to share:

1. No Uterus? No Say!
   https://www.youtube.com/watch?v=kzgJDZgQFSA
2. The Magical Birth Canal:
   https://www.youtube.com/watch?v=CNgwsT295G8
3. Body Inside My Body:
   https://www.youtube.com/watch?v=IufyKdrAQIY
4. Pamela Flanagin's Abortion Story | Pro life video story | Temecula Abortion story:
   https://www.youtube.com/watch?v=ee2S65RrDdg
5. Man roundhouse-kicks pro-life woman:
   https://www.youtube.com/watch?v=z7Sqtle5rZQ
6. Pro-Life vs Pro-Choice: It's A Baby
   https://www.youtube.com/watch?v=2y7bnaultow
7. Most Inspirational Pro-Life Video Ever Made - 60 Seconds:
   https://www.youtube.com/watch?v=DQvgjbRPjOk

Sources of Information and Counseling

Here are some additional sources of information concerning the topic of abortion – including some that may offer help in dealing with the aftermath of an abortion.

1. Rachel's Vineyard (post-abortion retreats)
   http://www.rachelsvineyard.org/
2. Project Rachel (hope after abortion)
   http://hopeafterabortion.com/
3. Life Site (Pro-life news) https://www.lifesitenews.com/
4. Priests for life http://www.priestsforlife.org/

A Former Planned Parenthood Director's Story

Former Planned Parenthood Director Reveals Why She's Desperate for People to Escape the Abortion Industry: https://www1.cbn.com/cbnnews/2018/october/former-planned-parenthood-director-reveals-why-she-rsquo-s-desperate-for-people-to-escape-the-abortion-industry

Works Cited:

1. Catechism of the Catholic Church. New York: United States Catholic Conference, Doubleday, 1994. Print.
2. Foote, Shelby. The Civil War a Narrative Fort Sumpter to Perryville. New York: Vintage Books, 1958. Print.
3. The Constitution of the United States.
4. The New American Bible. United States: Fireside Bible Publishers, 1987. Print.
5. Multiple internet sources (see footnotes, above).

Printed in Great
Britain
by Amazon